Jung, Psychology, Postmodernity explores points of confluence and, more often, contradictions between Jungian and postmodern ideas.

Throughout the book Raya Jones examines how personal meaning emerges in human activity. Jung addressed this in terms of symbol formation, with particular attention to dreams, myths, art and other fantasy productions. Postmodern psychologists tend to address issues of meaning in terms of people's self-understanding and identity construction, with a focus on self-positioning in actual conversation or on autobiographical narratives. Jones draws a line of critical comparison between postmodern psychology and Jung's descriptions of the symbolic dimension, myth and the structure of the psyche. The book culminates in an evaluation of Jung's psychic energy concept, for which there is no direct counterpart in postmodern psychology.

Jung, Psychology, Postmodernity is an original critique of two key moments in the history of psychology. It will be welcomed by Jungians, as well as psychotherapists and students of psychology.

Raya A. Jones is a social and developmental psychology lecturer at Cardiff University. She is a committee member of the International Association for Jungian Studies.

Jung, Psychology, Postmodernity

Raya A. Jones

Routledge
Taylor & Francis Group

LONDON AND NEW YORK

First published 2007 by Routledge
27 Church Road, Hove, East Sussex BN3 2FA

Simultaneously published in the USA and Canada
by Routledge
270 Madison Avenue, New York, NY 10016

Routledge is an imprint of the Taylor & Francis Group, an Informa business

© 2007 Raya A. Jones

Typeset in Times by Garfield Morgan, Swansea, West Glamorgan
Printed and bound in Great Britain by TJ International Ltd, Padstow, Cornwall
Paperback cover design by Jim Wilkie

This publication has been produced with paper manufactured to strict
environmental standards and with pulp derived from sustainable forests.

British Library Cataloguing in Publication Data
A catalogue record for this book is available from the British Library

Library of Congress Cataloging-in-Publication Data
Jones, Raya A.
   Jung, psychology, postmodernity / Raya A. Jones.
      p. cm.
   Includes bibliographical references and indexes.
   ISBN-13: 978-0-415-37948-9 (hardback)
   ISBN-10: 0-415-37948-2 (hardback)
   ISBN-13: 978-0-415-37949-6 (pbk.)
   ISBN-10: 0-415-37949-0 (pbk.)
   1. Jungian psychology. 2. Postmodernism—Psychological aspects. I. Title.
   BF173.J627 2007
   150.19'54—dc22
                                                    2007003131

ISBN 978-0-415-37948-9 (hbk)
ISBN 978-0-415-37949-6 (pbk)

Contents

Chapter 1

The relevance of Jung

Whenever, with our human understanding, we want to make a statement about something which in the last analysis we have not grasped and cannot grasp, then we must, if we are honest, be willing to contradict ourselves, we must pull this something into its antithetical parts in order to be able to deal with it at all.

(Jung, 1931a, CW 8: para. 680)

The conclusion to be drawn here is that an understanding of the nature of discourse as constituted by deadlocks of perspective means that it is the *failure* of agreement that needs to be displayed rather than an attempt to cover that disagreement over.

(Parker, 2005: 176)

Carl Gustav Jung (1875–1961), a Swiss psychiatrist and the founder of analytical psychology, engaged with matters that were central to the formation of psychology as a modern science in the early twentieth century (Shamdasani, 2003). In the long run, that science did not engage with Jung. A recent textbook by Harré (2005), *Key Thinkers in Psychology*, does not mention Jung. Rom Harré, himself a key thinker in postmodern psychology, has his own agenda in how he tells the history of psychology. In the traditional mainstream, Jung may be accredited with the distinction between introversion and extroversion, but his understanding of the typology was almost immediately overwritten. The distinction became a criterion for describing individual differences, understood as biologically based. To Jung, it signified different attitudes or stances underpinning human understanding (1921, CW 6). Jung's major contribution as a twentieth-century thinker is arguably not the personality types but his slant on the emergence of meaning in human activities. With the notable exception of Piaget (1962), who contends with Jung's account of symbol formation in his *La Formation du symbole chez l'enfant* (first published in 1946), the Jungian account was not picked up by psychologists as something worth bothering even to criticize. His effort to understand the meaning of meaning is best examined against the historical Project of Psychology, rather than evaluating its role in the history of the discipline as such. Several histories can be (and have been) told about how psychology became a modern science. But its project as a whole is best viewed as a culturally and historically specific expression of a quest for knowledge that transcends cultures and historical eras.

In eighth-century China, a Taoist passed by a Zen monastery, where a monk, Tsung Ching, kept a record of dialogues with the master Hui Hai (trans. Blofeld, 1962: 95). 'Is there anything in the world more marvellous than the forces of Nature?' asked the Taoist. Hui Hai replied, 'There is.' 'And what is that?' asked the Taoist. Hui Hai: 'The power of comprehending those natural forces.' Modern psychology, with its roots in eighteenth-century European philosophy, is more ambitious. It seeks to comprehend our own power of comprehending those natural forces. In 1781, Immanuel Kant contended,

> But though all our knowledge begins with experience, it does not follow that it all arises out of experience. For it may well be that even our empirical knowledge is made up of what we receive through impressions and of what our own faculty of knowledge . . . supplies from itself.
>
> (Kant, 1933[1781]: 41–2)

In late nineteenth-century Germany and Austria, experimental psychology emerged out of philosophy departments as an attempt to describe the workings of the cognitive faculty (Kusch, 1995). Although Jung's professional milieu, medical psychology, had a different history and (especially in the Germanic world) was instituted separately from the psychology that emerged out of philosophy departments, the same general project reverberates in his work. His theory of the collective unconscious and its archetypes attributes what the faculty of knowledge supplies from itself to biology and evolution. The same 'Kantian' project survived in various guises and permutations throughout the twentieth century. In the 1970s, cognitive psychology – the direct descendant of experimental psychology – was invigorated by the computer metaphor, likening the mind to an information-processing machine. Within a decade, critics within the academia, especially in social and developmental psychology, began to argue that all our knowledge, even our empirical knowledge, is made up of what language supplies from itself. This was the beginning of postmodern psychology.

During the last century, analytical psychology became established worldwide with its own institutional structure, several schools of thought, jargon, intellectual preoccupations and debates (see Kirsch, 2000) – and had little to do with psychology as pursued in university departments. An important post-Jungian work, James Hillman's (1975) *Re-Visioning Psychology*, makes no contact with the body of knowledge that I learned as a psychology student or with the re-envisioned psychology that I teach nowadays. Since the 1980s, there has been an upsurge of publications reinterpreting the old models of psychology and disseminating new ways of thinking about human nature. None that I know of acknowledges the richness of Jung's thought, let alone shows awareness of current directions in Jungian studies. Conversely, the steady outpouring of Jung-centred publications in the past couple of decades shows little awareness of how postmodernism impacted upon psychology. Christopher Hauke's (2000) *Jung and the Postmodern* does not mention a single postmodern psychologist (or any 'academic' psychologist, unless William James is counted as one). Like a mirror image, Steiner Kvale's (1992) edited volume *Psychology and Postmodernism* contains but one passing mention of Jung. In a single sentence, Jung is sandwiched between Freud on the one side, and Carl Rogers and B. F. Skinner on the other. The chapter's author points out that the postmodern standpoint reinterprets their systems, not as precise descriptions of the actual dynamics of human nature, but 'as models or metaphors that can serve as heuristic devices . . . for organizing client experiences' (Polkinghorne, 1992: 155). Jung would probably agree.

Jung was a man of science by virtue of being a medical doctor, but he was not a scientist, and described his concerns as a psychotherapist as differing from those of academic psychology at the time. Speaking in 1924, he spelled out the differences: unlike experimental psychology, analytical psychology does not 'isolate individual functions . . . and then subject them to experimental conditions for purposes of investigation' (1946, CW 17: para. 170). Instead,

> Our laboratory is the world. Our tests are concerned with the actual, day-to-day, happenings of human life, and the test-subjects are our patients, relatives, friends, and, last but not least, ourselves . . . it is the hopes and fears, the pains and joys, the mistakes and achievements of real life that provide us with our material.
>
> (Ibid.: para. 171)

Towards the end of the twentieth century, the experimental practices of scientific psychology came under severe attack from within the academia. As if echoing Jung's sentiment, though making a case for a variant of postmodern psychology, Mark Freeman (1997: 171) contended that the traditional categories of psychology leave out 'the living, loving, suffering, dying human being . . . human lives, existing in culture and in time'. But here the similarity ends. Jung claimed that analytical psychology is 'far more concerned with the total manifestation of the psyche as a natural phenomenon' than with isolated processes (1946, CW 17: para. 170). To him, the *total* manifestation includes the unconscious as well as conscious. This too distanced him from academic psychology and its materialistic biases, which meant ignoring the psyche. Jung pointed out that 'all modern "psychologies without the psyche" are psychologies of consciousness, for which an unconscious psychic life simply does not exist' – and therefore his 'psychology *with* the psyche', centred on the unconscious, would 'certainly not be a modern psychology' (1931a, CW 8: para. 658). It is also not a postmodern psychology, which means locating human consciousness in the materiality of discursive practices.

Although Jung was critical of academic psychologies, he shared their conviction that psychology ought to be a natural science. Recent critics within the academia have argued that by modelling itself on the natural sciences psychology has ignored, not only the hopes, fears, etc., of real life, but also its own cultural and historical specificity. The discontent found a voice (or voices, plural) in postmodernism. Ideas that had been bandied around in the humanities since the 1960s reached the social sciences a decade or so later. In this context, postmodernism means a form of social study that prompts the evaluative – and primarily qualitative – description of the particular, historical, local and discursive aspects of human life (e.g. Ryan, 1999). All strands of postmodern psychology embody this ethos, but their specific practices are shaped by diverse philosophical positions. Postmodern psychology is an aggregate of 'frameworks' – discursive, critical, narrative, rhetorical, sociocultural, dialogical – each with its own key figures, set of concerns and core premises that part-overlap, part-contradict those of other 'new' psychologies. There are admixtures of Foucauldian, feminist, psychoanalytical and Marxist orientations. During the 1990s, social constructionism emerged as the most distinctive philosophical standpoint, although its two major exponents – Rom Harré and Kenneth Gergen – fundamentally disagree with each other. The interrelation among postmodern psychologies could be described as 'not an agreement in opinions but in form of life' (Wittgenstein, 1953: §241). In his introduction, Kvale (1992: 1) points out that the 'very concept of a unitary discipline is at odds with postmodern thought'. Multivoicedness is hardly a postmodern peculiarity, however. Six decades earlier, Jung noted that 'there is not *one* modern psychology – there are dozens', commenting that this is 'curious enough when we remember that there is only one science of mathematics, of geology, zoology, botany and so forth' (1931a, CW 8: para. 659). What has been relinquished in the wake of postmodernism is the inclination to include psychology in that list of sciences.

It makes sense to speak of postmodern psychology in the singular insofar as it is a 'form of life' distinct from both modern psychology and from postmodernism elsewhere in the academia. It is distinguishable from both insofar as it must contend with the traditional natural-scientific model of the discipline. Whereas Jung saw in the modern academia an array of psychologies without the psyche, exponents of postmodern psychologies see in the modern lingering fallacies of psyche. The rhetoric of the new paradigm in psychology is replete with condemnations of old claims that the essence of human nature is pre-given, fixed and determines our being irrespective of history and culture. Jung held that man, like 'every animal . . . possesses a preformed psyche which breeds true to his species' and which 'enables a child to react in a human manner' (1954, CW 9I: para. 152). Kvale (1992: 1) described the postmodern break from traditional psychology as characterized by the 'decentring of the self, the move from the inside of the psyche to the text of the world' and from the 'archaeology of the psyche to the architecture of cultural landscapes'. Far from abandoning the archaeology of the psyche, Jung excavates its depths so as to find natural and prehistoric foundations for the cultural architectures of recent historical epochs. With little contact with each other, Jungian and postmodern psychologies resist each other's form of life. The impasse is not simply a case of schools of thought at loggerheads about some phenomena that they both observe. It is not a case of Jung saying 'The psyche is like this' and postmodern psychologists say, 'No, it's like that'. Postmodern psychology eschews the very assumption of a psyche, replacing it with views of subjectivity as an emergent property of discourse. The impasse is characterized by what Ian Parker describes as 'deadlocks of perspective' (apropos of Lacan and discursive psychology). I've made his conclusion one of the chapter's mottoes, for it captures my strategy in this critique.

A revision of Jung in the light of postmodern psychology or vice versa would do violence to both. We should acknowledge the existence of misalignment, the failures of agreement, which renders any integration of Jungian and postmodern psychologies a dubious enterprise. And why 'integrate'? Each psychology is thriving without apparent need for the other. That which might require some rescuing is the psychological issue of how human beings make their experiences meaningful. To paraphrase Jung (the chapter's other motto), if we are honest we must be prepared to pull that issue into its antithetical parts, and consequently be ready to admit that neither the Jungian nor the postmodern gives the full picture. We can't take the 'best of each' so as to make a whole – we don't know which bits are best, not having the full picture. If a synthesis should emerge, it might be 'a new content . . . standing in a *compensatory* relation to both' (paraphrasing Jung, 1921, CW 6: para. 825). First, we should try to pinpoint the various aspects of the thesis and antithesis at play. That is the task of this book.

Seeing the problem: the case of Stan's sister

It is customary to begin a scholarly work with a 'statement of the problem' – a section or chapter that exposes the failings of some established theory and in this way sets the scene for the writer's heroic rescue of Knowledge. It is a powerful narrative formula; but there are pitfalls. When identifying theoretical contradictions – as this book sets out to do – we inevitably think in terms of mutually exclusive categories. We are thus 'in danger of unconsciously resorting to disputation', as Plato warned (*Republic*, 1993: 454b). He attributes the seduction of sophistic disputation to people's 'inability to conduct the enquiry by dividing the subject matter into its various aspects. Instead their goal is the contradiction of statements at the purely verbal level' (ibid.: 454a). As a preventive measure, I would like to begin not with an argument but with a concrete 'anecdotal' case, through which the conceptual tensions giving rise to the arguments presented in this book become visible. It is based on child observations collected many years ago towards a vocational diploma, and was first told in Jones (2003a), where I called the child Martin; but 'Stan' allows the alliteration. This is the Case of Stan's Sister.

Four-year-old Stan was a large-built, sociable, physically active and confident boy, sometimes impertinent and a bully, but also chivalrous. He took great pleasure in helping girls tie their shoelaces, showing off his competence. He would flit from activity to activity trying to impress peers and staff with his power and 'magic' (a favourite word of his). Much of his play and conversations involved fantasies in which he was heroic. He was Superman or a lion, and told of fights with monsters, relishing in gory detail, but which he always fought for a noble cause. When I explained that I was in college when not in the nursery, he announced that he saw me there (he never visited the college), immediately adding that he 'saved a girl from an elephant and killed a big lion in college'. During January, *Star Wars* provided inspiration for much of his play. He was fond of making Lego spaceships, and talked a lot about Princess Leia, repeatedly telling people that he kissed her ('twice!'). Against that macho demeanour, there emerged some surprising behaviour. For about a fortnight, Stan obsessively dressed up in women's clothes from the dressing-up box. It was not role-play, he wasn't pretending to be anyone; he just liked to wear those clothes. He took a special liking to a certain red dress, and once I saw him chase a girl who wore it and force her to hand it over to him. The nursery staff found his cross-dressing highly comical, and eventually he seemed to be doing it for laughs. By early February the cross-dressing lost its earnestness, but something of its original intensity was transferred to plain curiosity about female underwear. One day the teacher led a group talk about the colours of the children's clothes. This prompted Stan to interrogate the girl sitting next to him about what she wore under her jumper. She showed him the shoulder strap of her vest. He insisted that it was a nightie and would not stand corrected. As the cross-dressing waned, an imaginary sister emerged (he had only an older brother). He mentioned her for the first time in my presence on 31 January. During outdoor play, the children kept running behind the building, which was forbidden. When they were called back by staff, Stan said excitedly, 'I can see my sister there!' Afterwards he kept drawing other children's attention to the forbidden place, insisting, 'I saw my sister there.' During February, Stan still mentioned Princess Leia, but usually as a teaser; e.g. telling me, '*You* didn't kiss Princess Leia!' There were no more mentions of her in March. Instead, he increasingly talked about his sister. He would claim to see her from the window, where the older children could be seen walking to the nearby primary school – saying, for instance, 'My sister goes to school, I don't care, I got a sister now' (15 March). He used her as a kind of trump card or one-upmanship: 'This is my sister, I'm not telling you her name!' he told me about a picture that he painted (21 March). A week later, he began saying that he was going to have 'a baby sister, a girl' (his mother was not expecting, as far as we knew). By the end of March the school term ended and so did my placement.

The same 'raw facts' of what Stan said and did can support contradictory theories about human nature. In one reading, it seems like a textbook case of classical Jungian theory. Jung submitted that the male personality has a feminine part, which he called anima; women have a corresponding animus (e.g. 1951, CW 9II). The anima sometimes appears as a sisterly voice in men's dreams. Stan's sister is like a dream projected onto his wakeful reality. At first she seems undifferentiated from his ego (it is he in female clothing), and sometimes projected externally onto a concrete icon supplied by popular culture, Princess Leia. Later she is externalized as the secret but realistic sister, who becomes even more plausible as a baby-to-be. There is a striking parallel with how Erich Neumann, following Jung, described ego development. He used the metaphor of the hero's journey. To quote from a textbook reviewing Neumann's theory,

> First, the hero/ego is trying to separate from the mother and the maternal environment. Second, the hero is trying to identify and discriminate the masculine and feminine sides of himself, so as to integrate them. Third, he is looking for values and modes of psychological functioning to offset and balance the over-directed and exaggeratedly conscious manner he has had to develop to break out of the embrace of the Great Mother. The ego has to behave in this over-stressed and stereotypically masculine way to free itself . . . The one-sided 'masculinity' can then be seen as necessary and inevitable, and in need of its opposite, namely the princess or similar feminine figure.
>
> (Samuels, 1985: 71)

Stan appears to be living through those precise stages in his heroic fantasies, exaggerated masculinity, imaginary girls he rescues, real girls he assists, Princess Leia and finally the Sister.

Stan was the only boy who displayed that pattern. The experiences that Jung attributed to the anima are probably ubiquitous – otherwise, his theory wouldn't ring true to so many analysts and their patients – but ubiquity alone is not evidence for the biologically hard-wired developmental programme that Jungian theory implies in some of its interpretations. The experiences in question could be due to growing up a boy, which involves building a masculine 'self' in opposition to a feminine 'other', for gender boundaries permeate cultural activities. Understood thus, the only universal aspect of Stan's ego development is what William James (1890: I, 278) described as 'one great splitting of the whole universe into two halves' made by each of us, *me* and *not-me*. Stan was filling up those halves with culture-specific content. Social constructionists Davies and Harré (1990: 47) posit that developing a self involves 'imaginatively positioning oneself as if one belongs in one category and not in the other (e.g. as girl and not boy, or good girl and not bad girl)'. Stan was acquiring, practising and testing storylines that go with masculinity versus femininity, and imaginatively inserting himself in those storylines.

Harré's positioning theory extends a line of thought that goes back to Jung's contemporary, George Herbert Mead, who attributed the genesis of the self to language-based social interactions (Chapter 2 expands). Mead (1934) suggested that children 'build a self' by entering various contexts of experience shared with other people, within which they acquire response repertoires that go with particular social categories. They practise those repertoires in social-role play. He viewed a child's imaginary companions as 'the imperfectly personified responses in the child to his own social stimulation, but which have more intimate and lasting import in his play than others of the shadowy clan' of make-believe characters (ibid.: 370).

Stan was learning to be a boy, not only by practising what boys do, but also through others' reactions to what he was doing and saying. The availability of the dressing-up box in the nursery school gave his experi-mentation with the feminine both the legitimacy and triviality of play. It relegated the pretty red dress to the 'not-me'. The nursery staff's laughter at the sight of the large boy in a frock taught him that the material culture of the feminine is barred to him, except as a joke. And he learned to use such 'jokes' as a source of power. He got staff's attention. He knew something I didn't (the sister's name), did something I didn't (kissing Princess Leia) and used the imaginary sister to challenge the ban on going behind the school. From this viewpoint, his gender identity is a disembodied social construction invested with the corporal body of a child who is instructed how to talk, walk and act like a 'man'.

The two interpretations of Stan's Sister seem mutually exclusive, though the 'failure of agreement' is accentuated by how I'm telling the story. Jung used a similar strategy in an introductory essay (1943, CW 7). He demon-strates how the neurosis of a certain patient could be explained equally well by applying either Freud's theory or Adler's. A Freudian explanation would attribute the neurosis to sexual desire. An explanation in accordance with Adler would attribute it to the 'will to power' (after Nietzsche), according to Jung. Jung shows that the contradictory explanations cannot both be correct – but he does not offer another explanation for the patient's neurosis (likewise, I shall not explain Stan's Sister any further). Instead, he reformulates the contradiction as a puzzle. How could Freud and Adler, both of them intelligent and astute, come up with contradictory theories? Concluding that Freud and Adler developed their theories on the basis of their own 'attitude-types' (extroversion and introversion), Jung launches his theory of the psychological types in general (see 1921, CW 6, for his full discussion). By implication, psychoanalytical (and Jungian) theories are akin to literary novels. They give a slant on human nature from their authors' subjective understanding, except that they are written in a 'scientific' genre that purports to impart objective knowledge. Jung and his followers talk of archetypes (such as the anima) as a scientific fact. To non-Jungian psychologists, it sounds like fiction. As seen, the 'fact' of Stan's anima is not seen at all when we interpret his behaviour by reference to a different set of concepts. How could we know which set of concepts is the correct one?

That question itself might be wrong, or at least open to interpretation. Psychology is first and foremost an empirical discipline. It seeks to describe human nature on the basis of systematic observations of what people actually do or say – as opposed to pure argumentation, as in philosophy, or by means of drama and fiction, as in the arts. But what counts as systematic empirical observations differs greatly. Different paradigms within psychology differ regarding how we may reliably collect empirical data (issues of methodology), and how to get from observation to inference and to defend our inferences (epistemology), inseparably from disagreements about the nature of human nature (ontology). Traditionally, the crucial criterion for the persuasiveness of any theory has been how its postulates are validated. To prefer either Jungian or social-constructionist readings of Stan's Sister on the grounds that it 'feels' correct would be like putting the cart before the horses. In actuality, other horses often pull the cart. Discoveries in the sciences are contingent on history, which is full of 'accidents and conjunctures and curious juxtapositions of events' (Butterfield, cited in Feyerabend, 1993: 9). New directions in psychology often seem influenced by biographical accidents and personal choices of charismatic thinkers. And those are made against the backdrop of wider historical conditions. Sociologists of knowledge attribute the emergence of new directions in the sciences in general to political and economic factors, and how those impinge upon scientists' own motives and priorities. Psychology is no exception (e.g. Kusch, 1995; Rose, 1985). The ethical-political issue of what is done with certain kinds of knowledge could influence what is seen as legitimate answers. Saying that Stan's imaginary sister is an anima projection perpetuates a knowledge elite – an 'us' who know what that statement means, because we read Jung, in the first instance; and, more selectively, a tightly controlled group of trained experts who are empowered to apply Jungian knowledge in psychotherapy. Many postmodern psychologists would put the question of how psychological knowledge is used or abused before the question of how it is validated.

When the topic of interest is the emergence of meaning, the epistemological problem does not lie in previous theories that 'got it wrong'. It lies in the impossibility of getting it right. The traditional criteria for an object of scientific study do not hold true for the self, as philosopher Charles Taylor (1989) pointed out. A scientific object must be taken objectively; that is, irrespective of its meaning to someone. It must exist independently of any description or interpretation of it, potentially be knowable in its entirety, and in principle could be described without reference to its surroundings. Jung recognized the problems inherent in applying those criteria to the study of the psyche. It is when we want definite, objectively verifiable, answers that we are confronted with what he regarded as the dilemma of modern psychology:

> One of the unbreakable rules in scientific research is to take an object as known only in so far as the inquirer is in a position to make scientifically valid statements about it. 'Valid' in this sense simply means what can be verified by facts. . . . [Modern psychology] does not exclude the existence of faith, conviction, and experienced certainties of whatever description, nor does it contest their possible validity . . . [but] completely lacks the means to prove their validity in the scientific sense.
> (Jung, 1948, CW 9I: para. 384)

The dilemma stems from a mismatch between what we may want psychology to do for us – to explain matters of faith, etc. – and what science permits us to do. 'One may lament this incapacity on the part of science, but that does not enable [the psyche] to jump over its own shadow' (ibid.: para. 384). The history of psychology could be told as an ongoing struggle with that dilemma, tackled from various different angles. Quite often the 'solution' has involved redefining the subject matter of psychology, sometimes by denying that there is a psyche trying to jump over its shadow. Social constructionism is a recent variation on the theme. To Harré (1998: 31), human behaviour rests on only two kinds of unobservable aspects: the 'domains of the vast network of interpersonal communicative acts that constitute the lived reality of human experience'; and material states and processes of the human organism, which enable the former but don't concern psychological inquiries. 'What is not needed is a neo-Cartesian mental realm of cognitive states and processes behind the public and private cognitive activities of real people' (ibid.: 31). Social constructionism allows us to link Stan's positioning of himself as the heroic rescuer of girls to the vast network of communicative acts of his milieu, but doesn't prompt us to ask how the imaginary sister came into being, and what it felt like to him to have her. It is like scientific thinking, which regards our private selves like 'bubbles on the foam which coats a stormy sea . . . floating episodes, made and unmade by the forces of the wind and water . . . their destinies weigh nothing and determine nothing' (James 1902: 495).

James countered the above caricature by pointing to the 'unshareable feeling which each one of us has of the pinch of his individual destiny' – a feeling that 'may be sneered at as unscientific, but it is the one thing that fills up the measure of our concrete actuality' (ibid.: 499). Jung's work could be viewed as a serious attempt to formulate a system of concepts towards the systematic description of how that unshareable feeling is manifest in concrete human productions, especially in fantasies. To many people worldwide, Jung was successful in that respect. Many of his followers have taken his practical concepts as scientific 'facts'. My position is critical, influenced by postmodern thinking about psychology. Jungian concepts such as the anima are at best convenient tools, at worst are mistaken for an explanation. The anima is a convenient label for a certain class of human experiences. We should ask whether it helps us to describe the psychological function of phenomena such as Stan's Sister – not ask whether such phenomena prove that an anima exists. The 'catch' is that if we find the specific concept useful, it impels us to explain observed phenomena by reference to it. Jung's own caveat is worth heeding. 'We must always bear in mind that despite the most beautiful agreement between the facts and our ideas, explanatory principles are only points of view' – but he can't resist adding, 'that is, manifestations . . . of the *a priori* conditions under which all thinking takes place' (1928, CW 8: para. 5).

The scientific method and poetic empiricism

Jung is most famous for the theory of archetypes. It is often misconstrued: 'My critics have incorrectly assumed that I am dealing with "inherited representations"' (Jung, 1964: 57). When not mistaken for inherited representations, archetypes are often treated as the actual motifs or themes, which Jung regarded as the surface manifestations of those tendencies. He complained that '"archetype" is often misunderstood as meaning certain definite mythological images or motifs' (ibid.: 57). It would be 'absurd to assume that such variable representations could be inherited', he stressed; the 'archetype is, on the contrary, an inherited *tendency* of the human mind to form representations of mythological motifs' (1961, CW 18: para. 523). Or, another definition – arguably his most important – archetypes are *'forms without content* . . . the possibility of a certain type of perception and action' (1954, CW 9I: para. 99). It is far from clear what Jung was actually dealing with. Not all analysts and scholars of Jung consider 'archetypes' as his most significant contribution, and among those who do engage with it, the concept is a matter for ongoing debate and reformulation. Commenting on the difficulties that 'psychologists of other persuasions' have with the

Jungian idea, Roger Brooke (1991: 157) points out that 'archetypes seem mysterious, deep, remote, frightening, and enchanting, and thinking about them remains equally murky and ambivalent'. From my corner as one of those psychologists, the problem is not that Jung did not provide a less ambivalent concept. There is little certainty at the cutting edge of science anyway. It is the *point* of postulating archetypes – the utility of the concept – which eludes us. Non-Jungian psychologists see little reason to clarify the idea of archetypes, because the very postulation seems redundant, a solution to a non-existing problem. 'Our' problem with Jung is that he claims to give us a psychology, yet violates our traditional expectations as to how a psychological theory ought to be validated.

Jung travels the Science road part of the way. Some of his speculations about the evolutionary origin of archetypes are incompatible with the subsequent scientific understanding of evolution and heredity, but that's not where Jung and Science part. His straying off the path begins with the leap of faith from observation to theory. He got the idea for the archetypes from clinical observations. 'For years I have been observing and investigating . . . dreams, fantasies, visions, and delusions of the insane. I have not been able to avoid recognizing certain regularities' (Jung, 1951, CW 9I: para. 309). Science could accept any theory, even ideas that initially seem to challenge common sense, but it requires more than hunches. It requires a systematic procedure that involves, among other things, an attempt to refute one's hunches. Otherwise it is like claiming to prove the existence of a ghost in the house by demonstrating that things go bump in the night, without eliminating other possibilities.

A few contemporary Jungians have tried to prove the innate origin of archetypes by using survey and statistical methods, but none of the studies that I know about checks out whether the findings could be explained also by alternative theories. Such efforts to rescue the credibility of Jungian ideas tend to misunderstand the *scientific method* even when they correctly apply methods that are routinely used in scientific investigations. The classic description of the scientific method is attributed to Karl Popper, whose important work on the topic was first published in German in 1934 and later translated by him into English. About the time that Jung was consolidating the theory of archetypes, Popper was criticizing the 'widely accepted view' according to which the logic of scientific discovery should be 'identical with inductive logic' (1958: 27). Inductive logic moves from '*singular statements* . . . such as accounts of the results of observations or experiments, to *universal statements*, such as hypotheses or theories' (ibid.: 27).

The problem with inductive logic is that we could never be sure whether the known singular instances reveal the full scope of the phenomenon they instantiated. Popper recommended that conclusions from a tentative new idea should be drawn by means of logical deduction. The internal consistency of the new theory would be ascertained by comparing the conclusions drawn from it with each other, and also with other ideas. The logical form of the theory – that is, 'whether it has the character of an empirical or scientific theory, or whether it is, for example, tautological' – should be investigated (ibid.: 32). The extent to which the new theory constitutes a scientific advance is determinable by comparison with other theories. Finally, the theory is tested through empirical applications of the conclusions derived from it. In the empirical application, predictions – called hypotheses – are deduced from the theory, especially such predictions as contradict or cannot be derived from the theory that the new one seeks to replace. If these are verified, 'then the theory has, for the time being, passed its test' (ibid.: 33).

Popper's description has been criticized on the grounds that scientific discovery might be contingent on historical accidents and on political and economic trends that favour certain directions (e.g. Feyerabend, 1993). Even if in practice Popper's ideal is compromised or wrong in parts, in his description we recognize modern science – and traditionally psychologists have worked to that ideal. Many still do. Jung chose a different path. Judged against the Popperian method, his *modus operandi* looks like a different form of life. Readers of Jung schooled in the humanities may recognize a hermeneutic approach in his interpretation of myths, ancient scripts, and patients' fantasies and dreams, but traditionally trained academic psychologists are not attuned to such methods. It is not clear to 'us' how he gets from observation to theory. He could be found guilty of inductive logic, for he progresses from accounts of particular dreams, hallucinations, myths and more, to the universal statement of archetypes. His transition from the observation of 'regularities' in clinical and mythological material to a full-blown theory is too rapid. He seems to be reading into the material his own expectations about the organization of the psyche, and there is little evidence of subjecting his idea to logical investigations such as Popper recommended. Jung's hypotheses have to be taken on trust. Believers see the evidence everywhere, and may understand the task of empirical research as a matter of compiling a catalogue of archetypal motifs. Jung characterized himself as 'an empiricist, not a philosopher' (1954, CW 9I: para. 149). To confuse matters, he derided empiricism on numerous other occasions, usually accusing Freud of such thinking. Strictly speaking, the doctrine of empiricism holds that theories ought to give a true account only of what is observable, and to eschew the reification of possibility or necessity. Clearly, Jung was not doing that – and neither did Freud or anyone who explains human behaviour by reference to hidden mental processes. Although modern science is empirical, unlike the philosophical doctrine of empiricism it aims to describe unobservable processes that explain the observable ones. Contesting the assumption of a continuum between direct observation and inference, van Fraassen (1980) proposed that the natural sciences should aim to provide theories that are empirically adequate, disregarding the question of whether the postulated entity really exists or not. Countless Jungian analysts and their patients find the unobservable entities postulated by Jung as empirically adequate, for these powerfully concur with personal experiences.

Jung's theory is a powerful narrative. It might be correct in the way that a literary novel, poem, musical piece or abstract painting is correct. That is, as a whole coherent unto itself, all its elements in perfect relation to each other. A scientific theory differs from a literary work, not only in the manner of its verification, but also in how we 'receive' its statements. The truth of a literary work lies less (if at all) in its accurate description of the world than in what it tells us about ourselves: 'we feel a poetic power rising naïvely within us. After the original reverberation, we are able to experience resonances, sentimental repercussions, reminders of our past. But the image has touched the depths before it stirs the surface' (Bachelard, 1994[1958]: xxiii).

Science too has a poetic core. To Popper, scientific discovery would be impossible without faith in ideas 'which are of a purely speculative kind, and sometimes even quite hazy; a faith which is completely unwarranted from the point of view of science' (1958: 38). However, whereas science seeks objective truths about the world (and human nature) by narrowing down possible interpretations, the truly poetic process creates its truths about our experience of the world through the multiplicity of overlain images and subjective connotations. Jung *amplifies*. His hypoteses are speculative explanations, not testable predictions. His most striking 'proof' for archetypes (in his view) was a patient's hallucination in which the sun was seen as having a phallus from which the wind comes (e.g. Jung, 1952, CW 5: para. 151). The imagery bore uncanny resemblance to a description that Jung found in an ancient Mithraic liturgy published in German a few years later. He argued that this imagery was too bizarre to have emerged by chance in unconnected sources. It later transpired that an earlier German publication was available, although Jung didn't know about it (e.g. Bair, 2003). Jung might have been duped; but even what he took at face value as a remarkable coincidence contradicts his theory. If the imagery were archetypal, surely it would be as common as images associated with the hero, mother, wise old man, etc. Rather than provide proof in the scientific sense, the solar phallus case was a turning point for Jung. Stumbling upon it was the catalyst that inspired his theory.

Making a similar point, Hillman (1983) commented that Jung uses the word 'empirical' to refer to a subjective process within him. 'The empirical event – the solar-phallus image in a patient – releases a movement in the mind setting off a hypothesis . . . as a poem may start in a concrete perception'; and like a poet, 'Jung returns ever and again to the concrete world of perceptions (cases, dreams, religious fantasies, ancient texts)' (ibid.: 32–3). Jung is empirical in accumulating concrete instances to support his ideas and in evaluating their practical therapeutic heuristics, but he is not empirical 'because the case is not the indispensable source of his insights or the place of their proving' (ibid.: 33).

Poetic empiricism is an oxymoron, coined here to capture the inherent tension in Jung's epistemology. Deleuze (1988) noted that science and poetry are equal forms of knowledge, irreducible to each other. Certain thresholds, such as aesthetic, 'mobilize knowledge in a direction that is different to that of science'; 'There are even ethical and political thresholds . . . certain prohibitions, exclusions, limitations, freedoms and transgressions are "linked to a particular discursive practice"' (quoting Foucault; ibid.: 20). Jung struggled with the incommensurability of these two practices in his work. In a talk on poetry, he endorsed the view of science and art as mutually exclusive: 'Art is by its very nature not science, and science by its very nature is not art' (1922, CW 15: 99). This was problematic for him, and an awareness of the conflict came to him in a typically Jungian manner. In 1913, whilst writing down some disturbing fantasies that he had, he wondered,

> 'What is this I am doing, it certainly is not science, what is it?' Then a voice said to me, 'This is art.' This made the strangest sort of an impression on me, because it was not in any sense my conviction that what I was writing was art.
>
> (Jung, 1989[1926]: 42)

Conversing with the inner voice, Jung resisted the idea that he was doing art. He felt that the voice 'had come from a woman. Obviously it wasn't science; what then could it be but art, as though those were the only two alternatives. That is the way a woman's mind works' (ibid.: 42). Having projected the source of his conflict – the belief in only two alternatives – onto the female 'other', Jung never resolved the question of what third alternative is there for him or any psychologist.

Psyche and discourse

Jung's psychology is not scientific, but human beings don't live by science alone. Our existence is made meaningful to us at a more basic and immediate level by means of poetic images and stories. The emergence of meaning by such means might seem like a topic of psychological interest *par excellence*, but traditionally it was studied by academic psychologists least of all. The neglect could be understood as a consequence of how the academic disciplines became divided in nineteenth-century German universities. The vested interests of influential professors played a key role in the allocation of psychology to the natural sciences (Kusch, 1995). A central figure in the administrative organization was Wilhelm Dilthey. Flew

(1979: 96) identifies Dilthey's project as 'examining human and social studies (*Geisteswissenschaften*)' and his major theme as 'the relations between lived experience, expression, and understanding (*Verstehen*): that is, understanding of the mind and how it directs and manifests itself in literature, language, and history'. Psychology had no room in Dilthey's vision for the *Geisteswissenschaften* (literally, sciences of the spirit) – and the young science of psychology had no room for 'spirit'. This had bearings on how Jung positioned his analytical psychology. A century later, the ethos of Dilthey's project would be recaptured in the practices of post-modern psychology. But given his professional and historical context, Jung was not inclined to regard psychology as anything other than part of the natural sciences.

Jung was well aware of the discrepancy between what he was doing with 'science', yet could not accept it as 'art', and didn't have the third alternative that has since opened in the postmodern social sciences. His ambivalent situation enters the language of his explanations. 'To interpret symbol-formation in terms of instinctual processes is a legitimate scientific attitude,' he states (1952, CW 5: para. 338). He concedes, 'I readily admit that the creation of symbols could also be explained from the spiritual side, but in order to do so, one would need the hypothesis that the "spirit" is an autonomous reality which commands a specific energy' (ibid.: para. 338). His psychology is centred on the hypothesis that the psyche is an auto-nomous reality commanding specific energy. Yet such a hypothesis 'has its disadvantages for the scientific mind', Jung comments – and declares, 'In accordance with my empirical attitude I . . . prefer to describe and explain symbol-formation as a natural process' (ibid.: para. 338). Nowadays it is 'discourse' that seems to function like an autonomous reality that com-mands specific power. 'Words and phrases have meanings that are organ-ized into systems and institutions, what Foucault . . . called "discursive practices" that position us in relations of power' (Parker, 1999: 6). The kind of explanation that Jung regarded as based in the legitimate scientific attitude would be understood as a *language game*. Wittgenstein (1953: §23) used that phrase to indicate that 'the "speaking" of language is part of an activity, or form of life'. The language game of scientism has empowered those who came up with explanations that use words like instincts, evolu-tion and (in Jung's context) energy, and discards explanations that use words like spirit as mystic twaddle. Language games are not 'games' but profoundly shape attitudes to our own and others' intellectual endeavours. Jung laboured to disengage his theorizing from religious mystification, seeking instead to explain psychological phenomena (including spirituality) as based in natural processes. The problem with Jung from the postmodern standpoint is not the same as from the standpoint of scientific psychology. Jungian ideas could not be readily assimilated into mainstream psychology due to a disparity between the criteria for scientific knowledge and how

Jung went about verifying his insights. Postmodernism involves a critique of what Lyotard (1984[1979]) called the pragmatics of legitimating scientific knowledge, privileging instead the pragmatics of narrative knowledge. But switching over to the latter in psychology does not legitimate Jungian ideas. His conception of the subject matter of psychology is grounded in that which the pioneers of the new paradigm have revised in their radical turn to 'discourse' (see, e.g., Henriques *et al.*, 1994[1984]; Parker, 1989; Gergen, 1994; Harré, 1998).

There is a difference between postmodern psychologies that draw chiefly on Wittgenstein's concept of language games and those drawing on Foucault's concept of discursive practices (Burkitt, 1999), but the consensus is that a meaning-world – or the world meaningfully – cannot exist outside discourse. Taking his cue from Foucault, Parker (1989) defines *discourse* as a system of statements. Such systems construct 'objects' such as stereotypes or attributions, which subsequently people talk about as if these objects really existed. 'This is how psychological . . . phenomena are created as individual "things"' (ibid.: 25–6). Derek Edwards and Jonathan Potter (1992) submit that what people commonly call attitudes, intentions, blame and so forth are created solely within conversational evaluations. Rather than assume that someone possesses a certain attitude (which may or may not be communicated verbally), they regard an attitude as a 'discourse action' inseparable from its verbal communication. When the same contention is applied to the self, it becomes redefined as the pronoun *I*: the self is 'an important grammatical operator . . . in much of what is taken to be meaningful discourse regarding persons' (Brown *et al.*, 1998: 85). The idea of the self as a grammatical operator is incommensurable with Jung's view of the self as arising from the natural psyche and encompassing 'both the experienceable and the inexperienceable' (1921, CW 6: para. 789).

The psyche whose precise structure was debated by Jung and Freud – and which discourse-centred psychologists reject – is not the same entity as the psyche described by Plato or Aristotle. The modern concept is mapped onto a notion of body–mind dualism, which was absent in Ancient Greece. The ancients thought in terms of inanimate versus animate entities. In their description, plants and animals also possess *psyche* but lack *nous*, the capacity for thought. Reviewing the history of concepts in modern psychology, Danziger (1997) suggests that the Greeks' *psyche* is not the same as its Latin translation, *anima*; the Roman concept is not the same as the medieval 'soul'; and none of these is the same as our modern conception of mind and self. The point is all the more poignant, for all three terms – psyche, anima, soul – have specific meanings in Jungian theory (which Danziger doesn't review).

Jung warned that we must be 'careful . . . with terminology, because it is historically coined and prejudiced' (1935, CW 18: para. 116). To him, the biases reproduced in careless terminology confound the real subject matter:

'The more you penetrate the basic problems of psychology the more you approach ideas which are philosophically, religiously, and morally prejudiced' (ibid.: para. 116). The implication is that there *is* an objective psyche, independent of its description by anyone, though impossible to observe directly. In contrast, the postmodern position holds that the very subject matter of traditional psychology reflects the prejudices that are built into specific languages. To say that language or (interchangeably) discourse is both the subject matter and medium for a psychological inquiry is not the same point that Jung was making when imploring his audience to be careful with terminology. From the postmodern standpoint, language is not just a means towards an end-goal. It is the very stuff that our goals are made of. Claims that Jung was presciently postmodernist should therefore be taken with the utmost circumspection. Such claims might be their authors' projections.

Contemporary sensitivities and preoccupations that are alien to Jung can indeed be found in current analytical psychology – in some (rare) instances making contact with postmodern psychology. Sue Austin (2005) draws upon feminist critical psychology, especially work by Valerie Walkerdine, towards her analysis of women's aggressive fantasies. Jung himself provided little by way of insight into what it is like to be a woman. There are other blind spots in Jung's theory. Although he made sweeping statements about societies and cultures – and some Jungians say that he was a 'culture theorist' – his outlook does not provide the best foundation for analysing political movements and historical transformations at the 'macro' level. Bringing his theory to bear on world events resulted in some peculiar commentaries by Jung, such as attributing the rise of the Nazis to the grip of a racial archetype, the Germanic god Wotan (1936, CW 10). Although his theory embodies preoccupations that nowadays are associated with postmodernism – such as a concept of the Other (Papadopoulos, 1984) and the disunity of the personality (Chapter 4 will expand) – Jung arrived at those from a different starting point and built upon them different conclusions than do postmodern psychologists. Jung was sceptical about the science of psychology, as seen; but he was sceptical for different reasons from those of its postmodern critics. Unlike those critics, Jung's disclaimers do not challenge the notion of a natural psyche. On the contrary, they reinforce it.

Jung begins his summative essay 'On the nature of the psyche' with a historical review (1954, CW 8). Up to the seventeenth century, psychology consisted of 'the enumeration of doctrines concerning the soul, but the soul was never able to get a word in as the object investigated', because thinkers spoke from their subjective viewpoint – an attitude that is 'totally alien' to the standpoint of modern science (ibid.: para. 343). The German word *Seele* (soul) is usually translated into English as 'psyche' when Jung writes about his own theory – perhaps because to anglophone ears, the word psyche sounded more scientific than soul. Jung's point was that, in the past, philosophers' theorizing was based on a naïve belief in the universal validity of their subjective opinions. As a modern science, psychology strives to describe the psyche objectively. Jung implies that nowadays psychology is more 'objective' inasmuch as it is not naïve any more: now we know that we can't escape our subjective situation. Having reviewed the objectivity of modern science as an improvement upon pre-Enlightenment thinking, he comments that we can never remove ourselves from the subjective situation: 'every science is a function of the psyche, and all knowledge is rooted in it' (ibid.: para. 357). Psychology as a science thus finds itself in an acute paradox, for 'only the psyche can observe the psyche' (1948, CW 9I: para. 384). Few other psychologies have made that concession, however. Understanding itself as a branch of biology, scientific psychology initially modelled its progress on physics. Modern physics became possible when a switch was made from values to abstract concepts – e.g. from describing the sensation of heat to the concept of temperature – and a similar revolution seemed imminent in the younger science of psychology. 'The most important general circumstances which paved the way for Galileian concepts in physics are clearly and distinctly to be seen in present-day psychology', Lewin (1935: 22) announced optimistically. 'The conquest over *valuative*, anthropomorphic classifications of phenomena on bases other than the nature of the mental process itself . . . is not by any means complete,' he admitted, but 'the chief difficulties are past' (ibid.: 22). For Lewin, psychology could be objective insofar as any trained psychologist, given the same observed facts, would arrive at more or less the same conclusion. The optimism was premature. On matters of meaning – matters that *matter* to people personally – objective science might be least helpful.

A different story of modern psychology is told in postmodernity. From a standpoint committed to the postmodern discourse of discourses, doctrines such as Jung's appear as based in a discourse where discourse didn't get a word in as the object of investigation.

Foucault attributed the creation of the modern 'soul' to historical conditions set in motion in the eighteenth century. Social institutions such as prisons, schools and clinics, and various discursive practices, place people in specific relations of power. Concepts such as psyche, subjectivity, personality, consciousness, etc. were created so as to carve out domains of analysing the post-Enlightenment soul, building upon it 'scientific techniques and discourses, and the moral claims of humanism' (Foucault, 1991[1975]: 30). Psychoanalytical practices inevitably reproduce certain power relations, such as the doctor/patient asymmetry and the doctor's duty of care. That is implicit in Jung's moral claim: 'We doctors are forced, for the sake of our patients . . . to tackle the darkest and most desperate problems of the soul, conscious all the time of the possible consequences of a false step' (1946, CW 17: para. 170).

Jung neither doubted the reality of mental illness nor challenged the legitimacy of professional expertise. He described analytical psychology as 'an eminently practical science' that does not 'investigate for investigation's sake, but for the immediate purpose of giving help. We could even say that learning is its by-product, but not its principal aim, which is again a great difference from what one understands by "academic" science' (ibid.: para. 172).

In this book, the strands of postmodern psychology selected for the comparison with Jung do investigate for investigation's sake. Despite the imperative to get it right for the patients' sake, the practitioner ethic fosters a greater tolerance of interpretative tools and heuristics, such as analogies and anecdotes, than is the case in science, which prefers tight arguments and hard evidence. The scientist ethic puts getting the theory right before applying it in practice. Practical goals tend to be regarded as a moral obligation – good theories ought to be put to the common good – but, to the scientist, the crucial question is how good the theory is. The goodness of the theory is judged less by its practical applicability than by how well it fits reality (as we see it). The 'reality fit' criterion applies also in inquiries premised on the postmodernist assumption that our realities are created within discursive practices. It is expected that researchers would provide a faithful description of practices that exist independently of the research. The moment that we give something a meaning, 'we are placing it in the logical space of reasons, of justifying and being able to justify what one says' (Sellars, cited in Rorty, 1980: 389). Rorty used Sellars' statement to amplify his own argument against the assumption of essential truths that could be described by scientists or philosophers. He proposes to view '*conversation* as the ultimate context within which knowledge is to be understood' and to regard knowing as 'a right, by current standards, to believe' (ibid.: 389). Jung, commenting that in psychology we lack an observation point outside the psyche, reflected that this doesn't rule out 'the possibility that the atomic physics of the future may supply us with the said Archimedean point' (1948, CW 9I: para. 384). He might have said it wryly or put too much faith in physics, but either way his comment does not revoke the right to believe in a psyche that exists separately of our statements about its behaviour. This right is revoked in the social constructionist view that people are 'for ever producing and reproducing their own minds and the societies in which they live' in flows of discursive action (Harré, 1998: 15). It is from the scientist ethic that social constructionists tend to query the nature of the phenomena studied by psychology. Harré concedes, 'Of course our individual powers, skills and abilities are grounded in something continuing, and their implementation requires the working of causal mechanisms. But none of this is psychological' (ibid.: 15). At stake is the definition of *psychology*.

Describing progress in the natural sciences, Feyerabend (1993) sketched two overlapping circles, labelled 'old theory' and 'new theory' respectively.

The area of their overlap, Domain D, represents 'the problems and facts of the old theory which are still remembered and which have been distorted so as to fit into the new framework' and create a demand for increasing its own content (ibid.: 157). Since the 1980s, the rhetoric of the new psychology heralded its own emergence as akin to paradigm shifts in science. The rhetoric of the 'new' problematizes the 'old' and in this way has opened up an academic niche for itself. To date, a shift in dominance of paradigms has not happened. Cognitivism not only continues to flourish unperturbed by postmodernist critique but is invigorated by advances in neuroscience. The postmodern paradigm has formed a mainstream of its own, with strongholds in several British universities. It lately acquired the generic label of 'critical social psychology' (e.g. Tuffin, 2005). The entrapment of a Domain D is perhaps inevitable when a new theory is understood as an improvement upon an older one. What should be avoided is the kind of rhetoric that defends the legitimacy of one viewpoint mainly by demolishing another. Initially, the new psychologies created a niche for their form of social study by constantly reminding us of the serious problems inherent in the old paradigm. For example,

> In the [old view], committed to the assumption of the primacy of individual being, human nature is biological, it is lived psychologically, and therefore is social. In [ours], committed to the assumption of the primacy of social being, human nature is cultural, it is lived socially, and therefore it is psychological.
>
> (Varela and Harré, 1996: 317)

Introducing their own commitment to social primacy as a 'dynamic conception of human nature' (ibid.: 317), Varela and Harré implicitly index biologically oriented viewpoints as embodying a static conception – an odd characterization of psycho-*dynamic* perspectives (Jones, 2002a). The two conceptions of human nature are dynamical, but differ in terms of *where* they seek the dynamics, an inner/outer dimension. Forever pitching 'theories' against each other, we slide into disputation (cf. Plato) and lose or never gain sight of the dimensions along which various claims are polarized. Identifying conceptual discontinuities is only part of the story, a case of seeing the glass as half empty. There are also continuities of ideas across the ages of Western thought, the half-full glass. Continuities exist, not solely as a consensus about something, but also by virtue of the ideas that are seen as fit to contest.

Attributing that which the faculty of knowledge supplies from itself to biology and evolution, Jung held that fragments of things seen, heard and so forth, are rearranged by the mind according to an internally imposed order. He reasoned that that order must arise from the inner structure of the psyche itself. 'For it is the function of consciousness not only to recognize and assimilate the external world through the gateway of the senses, but to translate into visible reality the world within us' (1931b, CW 8: para. 342). He proposed that some of the factors influencing a person's conscious situation are collective rather than personal, and are expressed in 'material primarily derived from the *collective unconscious*' (1921, CW 6: para. 746). Jung regarded the theory of the collective unconscious as his greatest achievement, and it is certainly the most original aspect of his psychology. It is the cornerstone of analytical psychology, something that any Jungian analyst or scholar must contend with at some point and in some way. It is not directly the preoccupation of this book, but enters its themes obliquely. The immediate preoccupation is captured, in a small way, in the discrepant uses of the word *collective*. In Jungian use, 'collective' refers to something that everyone has by virtue of evolution and biology, like having a brain. In the social sciences, 'collective' implies a joint activity or something created by virtue of the co-ordinated actions of two or more people, like playing a duet or symphony. Some critics of social constructionism from other postmodern viewpoints argue that, despite 'the primacy of the social, there is a mind at work in the use of social experience and material, and that mind has an active, transforming function' (Dodds *et al.*, 1997: 497). Jung could be said to describe the active transforming function of the mind; but when the primacy of the social is taken as indisputable, it is difficult to consider his description as a remedy for the shortcomings of social constructionism. That's the site of tensions that this book as a whole seeks to examine.

Scholarly critiques also have agendas, and I want to make mine clear. Gergen (1997) delineates three kinds of postmodern critiques of psychology. A 'social analytic' line of critique is concerned with how social processes shape the profession's assumptions about its subject matter, its methodologies and, ultimately, the conclusions that we may reach about human nature. An 'ideological unmasking' points to the ramifications for society that certain ways of describing and explaining human action have. Its more extreme manifestations are associated with the movement of critical psychology (where 'critical' alludes to Marxism), which is centrally concerned with the analysis of how power is used or misused in psychology and in society generally. The third line identified by Gergen, 'literary and rhetorical deconstruction' – which best describes my strategy – examines how the texts of psychology are structured, what are their implicit metaphors of mind or person, and how they sustain certain worldviews through their narratives. Consider the following piece of text:

> The symbol-creating process substitutes for the mother the city, the well, the cave, the Church, etc. . . . Because the incest taboo opposes the libido and blocks the path to regression, it is possible for the libido to be canalized into mother analogies thrown up by the unconscious. In

this way the libido becomes progressive again, and even attains a level of consciousness higher than before.

(Jung, 1952, CW 5: para. 313)

It is not important here to decipher the above or ponder its truth (Chapter 5 will return to that). The statement has the authoritative tone of a substantiated scientific explanation. In the lengthy discussion surrounding the excerpt, Jung draws subtle distinctions between Freud's explanation and his own. But if we don't participate in the language game that treats the libido as if it really exists, the whole debate seems pointless, reminiscent of counting angels on a pinhead, and Jung's finest lucubration becomes unintelligible. At this point the critic's agenda would come into play. Some social constructionists use the unintelligibility of libidinal explanations to discredit anything that Freud (and consequently Jung) said as 'a freakish version of causal powers . . . and a temptation to hermeneutic fascism' (Varela, 1995: 374). In general, the method of deconstruction is attributed to Jacques Derrida, who showed that any meaning structure could be dismantled in infinite regress. In postmodern psychology, it became most commonly associated with polemical demolition (cf. Hepburn, 1999) – that is, at the service of ideological unmasking. When ideological unmasking is the critic's real agenda, the critique forfeits critical distance. Demolishing one ideology is undertaken so as to make room for another, the truth claims of which are uncritically endorsed. My agenda is different. Deconstructing passages such as the above excerpt should lead to a reconstruction of meaning. Does anything worthwhile remain in what Jung is saying when we do away with the libidinal metaphor? Can it be translated intelligibly into the discourses of postmodern psychology? Do reasons for even attempting such a translation arise within those discourses? Such questions have brought about the themes of this book.

'So what is the relevance of Jung?'

This chapter has outlined some (arguably) good reasons for querying notions that Jung's psychology is either scientific or postmodern. It is something else. There are also not-so-good reasons for dismissing Jung, based in ignorance and misconceptions about him and his thought. 'We American psychologists are brought up to think of Jung as a mystic,' disclosed Rychlak (1984: 34). This applies also to British psychologists, in my experience. Jung is almost always a personal discovery, a passion kindled by extracurricular reading. In a typical syllabus, he features as an embellishment on a historical review of Freud; and, at best, is given credit for the personality types. Several factors converged so as to bring about his virtual exclusion. The Freudian story, which depicts Jung as a dissenting disciple, persisted when the behaviourists 'debunked' Freudianism. It was retained when behaviourism itself gave way to cognitivism as the dominant view-point. By the time that postmodern critics of cognitivism appeared on the scene, Jungianism was too remote even to criticize. Meanwhile Freud was 'rediscovered', partially reinvented, by luminaries of postmodernism, and consequently arrived also in certain contexts of postmodern psychology. Jung remains excluded. Besides Freudian prejudices and misconceptions about Jung that were carried over, the rise of the new paradigm during the 1980s, with its heightened moral and political sensitivities, coincided with highly publicized allegations of Jung's Nazi sympathies and anti-Semitism. Some of the allegations are unfounded (Bair, 2003; Shamdasani, 1998), but the scandal placed Jung off-bounds for most psychologists at the forefront of postmodern psychologies, such as Michael Billig (1999: 6): 'For political reasons I cannot allow myself to read Jung with pleasure.'

Reading Jung is difficult with the best of intentions. The vast sweep of his eclectic knowledge results in verbose density and opacity. There are books that reliably disseminate Jungian theory at a basic level (my recommendations are Stein, 1998, and Bennet, 1983) – but any simplification forfeits what the historian Petteri Pietikäinen (1999) aptly called the kaleidoscopic nature of Jung's psychology. Any reading of Jung involves navigating his voluminous writings, not only in terms of what is actually read, but also by selecting threads that attract the particular reader. To different readers, Jung 'talks' differently. Consequently, there is a vast body of Jung-related publications, many of which have little in common with each other, and some have a dubious relation to Jung's actual work. Pietikäinen notes 'a profusion of "book-length commercials of Jungian therapy" and "pseudo-religious apologetics"' (ibid.: 27). There are also works of academic excellence within analytical psychology (see, e.g., Papadopoulos, 2006), but they tend to be too esoteric for the uninitiated. All that doesn't help to make an interest in Jung a respectable pursuit for an academic. Some of us pursue nonetheless. There are scholarly studies by non-analysts, too numerous to list here – some will be cited in the course of the book – that compare Jung with various thinkers (including Pietikäinen's comparison of Jung and Cassirer) or apply Jungian ideas in literary, film and religious studies. Jung is often listed as a myth theorist and is sometimes studied as such. In and out of the academia, 'Jung' has become a kind of brand name that can be stamped on a variety of products.

Since Jung regarded himself as first and foremost a psychologist, it is ironic that he is least studied by psychologists. For the 'typical' psychologist, the above barriers to engaging with Jung's work are compounded by misconceptions and bafflement about what he was actually saying. Despite Jung's preoccupation with some of the central concerns of the early science of psychology, his pivotal concepts cannot be readily mapped onto the sequences of questions-and-answers that constitute psychology as taught and practised in university departments. When Jung 'speaks' to scholars –

in any discipline – his ideas are made rational by interlacing them with other ideas that already make sense to us, including ideas that Jung didn't know about or couldn't have known about. When we engage in such reconstruction of Jung, we practise a kind of poetic empiricism: the encounter with the Jungian text sets off associations and opens up possibilities for understanding, and we may return time and again to his work to confirm our own hypotheses. We place a 'Jung' in a narrative of our own making. This book is no exception. It weaves a sort of thread through continuities and discontinuities between Jungian and postmodern psychological ideas.

Jung's historical significance is not a measure of his influence on academic psychology (he didn't influence it), but the extent to which certain attitudes, assumptions and dilemmas that characterized twentieth-century psychology as a whole became focalized in his work. Approaching Jung historically does not mean merely identifying whence he got his ideas. Ernst Cassirer (1946[1925]: 27) advised: 'genuine historical reflection . . . must strive . . . to find those "pregnant" moments in the course of events where, as in focal points, whole series of occurrences are epitomized'. He concludes,

> So historical conception . . . is characterized by the fact that through it a thousand connections are forged by one stroke; and it is not so much the contemplation of particulars as an awareness of such relationships that constitutes the peculiar historicity, or what we call the historical significance of facts.
>
> (Ibid.: 28)

From the late nineteenth century through to the present day, one of the most abiding issues in psychology has been its own definition. What do we do when we say that we are doing psychology? The dilemma was acutely expressed in Jung's deliberations about what he was doing – if 'it wasn't science; what then could it be but art?'. Postmodern psychology offers another alternative: a form of social study based mostly on qualitative analyses of discursive productions. Yet when making the shift from psyche to discourse, something seems lost from sight or difficult to articulate. Whether in the last analysis we agree or disagree with Jung's answers, looking at his questions is relevant in this ongoing quest of ours to comprehend the power of comprehension and our own nature.

Chapter 2

Symbolic and dialogic dimensions

[The *symbolic attitude*] is only partially justified by the actual behaviour of things; for the rest, it is the outcome of a definite view of the world which *assigns meaning* to events, whether great or small, and attaches to this meaning a greater value than to bare facts.

(Jung, 1921, CW 6: para. 819)

The actually performed act . . . somehow knows, somehow possesses the unitary and once-occurring being of life; it orients itself within that being, and it does so, moreover, in its entirety – both in its content-aspect and in its actual, unique faculty.

(Bakhtin, 1993: 28)

One summer I assisted in a play scheme for schoolchildren, organized by parents in a village school. One day, one of the scheme's leaders, Betty, brought along her 20-month-old daughter, Louise (not their real names). Betty organized art activities for the children enrolled on the scheme, and decided that Louise too should do something 'creative'. Having left Louise standing on the teacher's chair, with me guarding her, she went to cut out coloured foil into many small pieces, and then brought those along with glue and paper over to the desk. Betty carefully explained the sticking procedure to Louise, who paid no attention. Louise was more interested in dipping her finger in the jar and tasting the glue. Worrying that it might be toxic, I coaxed her to dip foil pieces instead. Ignoring me, she sombrely ran her forefinger on the foil pieces. Her mother went to find safer glue. Meanwhile, Louise thoughtfully examined the little black balls that had formed on her fingers as the glue dried. Then she tried to remove foil pieces that Betty had glued to the paper, and were now in various stages of bonding. Betty returned with a pot of glue that had to be pressed down onto the paper, and instructed Louise to 'bang' it on the paper. The pot was too large for Louise to hold. I dabbed a few spots of glue on the paper, and encouraged her to place foil pieces on those spots. *All of a sudden, Louise scooped up as many foil pieces as she could and distributed them all over the paper in a sweeping motion. She smiled at the brief cloud of colourful pieces, and watched intently as a shower of them descended all the way down to the floor*. Her mother promptly abandoned the activity and tidied everything away.

The sweeping scoop and confetti-like shower, in its entirety of unexpected dramatic action and spectacular result, seems attuned to her emancipation from the overbearing adults. Louise finally did what *she* wanted with those foil pieces. Defining the symbolic dimension of creative acts may begin at this point, in what Bakhtin described as the act that somehow knows, somehow orients itself within being in its entirety. It would not suffice, however. All Louise did was to explore tactile and visual properties of her material environment. Her action was not symbolic play in the conventional sense of the term, because there was no make-believe. If an older Louise pretended to throw confetti in a wedding, her make-believe would not necessarily be symbolic as Jung defines it. According to Jung, a symbol is 'the best possible formulation of a relatively *unknown* thing . . . standing for something that is only divined and not yet clearly conscious', which 'depends chiefly on the *attitude* of the observing consciousness' (1921, CW 6: paras. 817, 818). In turn, attitude is defined as a state of readiness in which there is 'a definite combination of psychic factors or contents, which will either determine action in this or that definite direction, or reacts to an external stimulus in a definite way' (ibid.: para. 687). There was an attitude in Louise's action, and the action had emotional signifi-cance as indicated by her smile, but the assignment of a definite meaning to it is mine. That which Jung calls the *symbolic attitude* involves a conscious-ness that assigns meaning to the act that 'somehow knows' – and in this case the assignment of meaning is mine. For meaning to emerge, then, there must be two consciousnesses and an oscillation between them (which could be different states of the same person). That is where the definition of the dialogic dimension may begin. A borrowed anecdote may illustrate.

The Jungian analyst Elisabeth Urban (2003) tells how, during a clinical session, a troubled six-year-old boy drew a picture of a head without a body. Urban put it to him that he felt like nobody, with which he agreed. Since he also drew figures with bodies, the no-body drawing seems like an act that 'somehow knows', and the analyst was acting like a Socratic midwife, helping him to articulate something about himself that he already knew but perhaps couldn't articulate (see also Bovensiepen, 2002). Put another way, the analyst's interpretation helped along a shift of conscious-ness in the child by amplifying a way of seeing himself. There is more to this example, however. The drawing as an act-oriented-to-being is called into being, not only in its concrete content, but in its content *plus* how it is perceived *plus* a set of ideas and associations supplied by a particular language – in this case, the English language and the Jungian discourse. Another psychologist might interpret the production of the drawing as regression to an earlier developmental stage. Although this too would connect the drawing to the child's emotional problems, it would not see the pictorial content as expressing his self-image. Specific associations built into particular language create a readiness to make certain connections (Wittgenstein, 1953). The no-body pun of the child's drawing cannot be translated into Hebrew, for instance.

The premise of this chapter is that a 'meaningful' act unfolds in terms of two inseparable dimensions, interrelated like the horizontal and vertical axes of a rectangle. In some rectangles the horizontal is greater than the vertical; in other, it is the other way around. Sometimes we may want to focus on the symbolic unfolding, sometimes on the dialogic. Those foci are not rival theories about the causes of some observed behaviour. When seeking theories that may shed light on the respective psychological processes, we do get caught between rival viewpoints about the nature of human nature. Their foci of convenience are often prompted by a particular worldview. An examination of Jung's approach to symbols should consider what it excludes as well as what it includes. From the outset, he strictly separates the symbolic from the 'semiotic', which he defines as the signalling of known things. But when the formative absences in his theorizing about the symbolic are pulled together, like hidden threads, they do not result in his notion of the semiotic. Rather, they constellate into what is placed below under the label 'dialogic'. This shadowy other of Jungian theory is visible in postmodern psychology, especially in social constructionism.

Defining the symbolic

Jung's definition of symbol (henceforth, Definition) is one of the longest entries in the glossary appended to 'Psychological types' (1921, CW 6). It makes four main propositions.

First, a symbol is not a sign:

> An expression that stands for a known thing remains a mere sign and is never a symbol. . . . Every psychic product, if it is the best possible expression at the moment for a fact as yet unknown or only relatively known, may be regarded as a symbol, provided that we accept the expression as standing for something that is only divined and not yet clearly conscious.
>
> (Ibid.: para. 817)

Second, whether or not something is symbolic depends, not on its formal content, but on the *symbolic attitude* of the person interacting with specific content, i.e. a consciousness that assigns meaning and value to what is seen, heard and so forth.

Third, a symbol is a function of the dynamic structure of the psyche as specified by Jung. The Definition relates the symbol to the ego and the functions of consciousness (thinking, feeling, sensation and intuition). It attributes symbol formation to flows of psychic energy, and links to Jung's view of the psyche as composed of paired opposites.

Fourth, a symbol serves a *transcendent function* by standing in a complementary relation to elements of the psyche that are in opposition to each other. Jung discussed the transcendent function in an essay bearing this title, which was written in 1916 but remained unpublished until discovered by students of the C. G. Jung Institute 42 years later. It was then published 'with all its imperfection, as an historical document', as Jung says in a Prefatory Note (1958, CW 8: para. 67). Its topic, Jung noted in 1958, is 'the universal question: How does one come to terms in practice with the unconscious?' He adds, 'This is the question posed by the philosophy of India, and particularly Buddhism and Zen. . . . For the unconscious is not this thing or that; it is the Unknown as it immediately affects us' (ibid.: para. 68).

The words 'known' and 'unknown' are often used as synonymous with 'the conscious' and 'the unconscious', but the semantic choice is not innocuous. The vocabulary of conscious/unconscious implies mental realms, set as if apart from the world, like a filing cabinet with some drawers locked. This might seem intuitively correct in view of ample evidence for repressed or simply forgotten personal knowledge (which must be stored somehow). It is reinforced by Freud's vivid analogy, which invites us to imagine the unconscious as if it were

> a large entrance hall, in which the mental impulses jostle one another like separate individuals. Adjoining this entrance hall there is a second, narrower, room – a kind of drawing-room – in which consciousness, too, resides. But on the threshold between these two rooms a watchman performs his function: he examines the different mental impulses, acts as a censor, and will not admit them into the drawing-room if they displease him.
>
> (Freud, 1974[1917]: 336)

Jung, in 'The transcendent function', implicitly endorses the notion of the unconscious as a depository when he lists various types of contents that belong there: 'all elements that are too weak' to reach the threshold of consciousness; material incompatible with conscious inhibition that 'sinks into the unconscious'; 'all the forgotten material of the individual's own past'; 'all the inherited behaviour traces constituting the structure of the mind'; 'all fantasy combinations which have not yet attained the threshold intensity' (1958, CW 8: para. 132). Jung's main point is that the unconscious and the conscious behave in a complementary or compensatory manner towards each other. The implicit anthropomorphism becomes explicit towards the essay's end: 'It is exactly as if a dialogue were taking place between two human beings with equal rights, each of whom gives the other credit for a valid argument' (ibid.: para. 186). He points to phenomena of 'hearing voices' so as to posit the idea of an inner dialogue as a psychological fact. The picture of a person-like unconscious, the inner 'other' with whom 'I' converse, retains the positivist undertones of the Freudian analogy. It implies that there is positively something else there, which 'I' (ego) doesn't know. The dialogue analogy has a postmodern appeal to it, but arguably it confounds a more crucial issue that Jung was addressing in that essay. Instead of asking why some knowledge *about* self and world is inaccessible to someone (which remains a valid question), in this instance Jung asks how knowledge *of* self-in-world is possible at all.

By introducing the essay with references to Buddhism and Zen, Jung invites us to think along different lines: 'the unconscious is not this thing or that; it is the Unknown'. Something that is not known is still a definite thing, though. Integrating Jungian theory with existential phenomenology, Brooke (1991: 153) points out that human beings are 'always attuned to the world in some way. Feelings, emotions and moods are thus always situated. More than that they always disclose one's situation in a manner that is immediately (i.e. without cognitive mediation) intelligible'. This redraws the conscious/unconscious boundary in terms of the presence/absence of cognitive mediation (i.e. thinking). If feeling, intuition and sensation also are regarded as functions of consciousness (as Jung regarded them), 'attunement' as a whole is only one side of the coin. On this side, there are both things that I can think about and things that I can't, yet am aware of by other means. On the other side, there is nothing – but it is nothingness that has definite implications for attunement. This is implied in another analogy provided by Jung, in which he likens the transcendent function to complex numbers. Complex numbers are composed of real and imaginary numbers; similarly, the 'psychological "transcendent function" arises from the union of conscious and unconscious contents' (1958: para. 131). An imaginary number is a non-existent quantity involving the square root of a negative number. Unlike Freud's censor or Jung's dialogue analogies, this analogy doesn't give us a concrete image to hold in the imagination. We may look elsewhere, as Jung does in another context (regarding synchronicity, to do with meaningful coincidences). He cites in full the following passage from the Taoist text, *Tao Te Ching* (albeit in a different translation):

Thirty spokes
Share one hub.
Adapt the nothing therein to the purpose in hand, and you will have the use of the cart. Knead clay in order to make a vessel. Adapt the nothing therein to the purpose in hand, and you will have the use of the vessel.

> Cut out doors and windows in order to make a room. Adapt the nothing therein to the purpose in hand, and you will have the use of the room. Thus what we gain is Something, yet it is by virtue of Nothing that this can be put to use.
>
> (Lao Tzu, trans. 1963: 67)

Jung comments, '"Nothing" is evidently "meaning" or "purpose", and it is only called Nothing because it does not appear in the world of the senses, but is only its organizer' (1951, CW 8: para. 920). His interpretation might be biased by the translation of *tao* as 'meaning'. The word is usually translated into English as 'way', though probably neither translation is wrong. Lu K'uan Yü (1961: 243) lists the various words applied in his own translation of *tao*: 'road, way, path, doctrine, truth, self-nature, the absolute'. The translation of *tao* as 'meaning' allows Jung to read into the passage an allusion to what the faculty of knowledge supplies from itself (cf. Kant). Symbols are real things with causal effects, leading to human action that has real consequences in the world, but they don't exist (as symbols) in the world of the senses. It is 'quite impossible to create a living symbol, i.e. one that is pregnant with meaning, from known associations' (Jung, 1921, CW 6: para. 817). All the visual, verbal and other components of the symbol are things seen, heard, etc. (i.e. known), yet to function *as a symbol* their juxtaposition must be seen as meaningfully organized into a whole. This organizer, the psyche or mind, is a 'nothing', for it does not exist in the world of the senses, yet it is the active producer of meaning. Lao Tzu's point was different, simpler and closer to the interpretation of the 'transcendent function' laboured here. The practical use (meaning) of the cart, vessel or room as containers is paradoxically made possible by creating an empty space, a nothing-therein. Like the spokes that share one hub, the paradox of gaining something by virtue of nothing reappears in various different instances. Derrida famously demonstrated how gaps or absences in a text are as formative of its meaning as what is actually said.

The transcendent-function idea attributes the formation of symbols to the 'union' of conscious and unconscious contents. This could be represented by means of a formula: $S = f(K, U)$. The formula is shorthand for saying that symbol S is an outcome of the interaction between a known factor K and an unknown factor U. Viewed thus, symbol and sign (in Jung's idiom) are not in the same category order. A sign is a known thing, a K factor, but symbol is neither known nor unknown, for it is the outcome of their interplay. The algebra is plain enough, but Jung didn't speak in formulae. In his writings, the expulsion of the semiotic from the conception of the symbolic is managed rhetorically. In the 1921 Definition, the word *symbol* is surrounded with evocative words such as 'living', 'pregnant with meaning', 'divined', 'impossible to create', 'numinous' and 'psychological'. Not much surrounds the word *sign* besides 'known' and 'allegoric'. Since a symbol is a living thing, it could be dead; a sign is neither. A symbol is organic, natural and thus psychological, whereas a sign is a mere custom or convention, and therefore of little concern in psychology (the rhetoric implies). As early as 1907 (CW 3), Jung contrasted his use of the terminology of symbolism with notions of allegorical contents. 'Allegory, for us, is the intentional interpretation of a thought, reinforced by images, whereas symbols are only indistinct, subsidiary associations to a thought, which obscure it rather than clarify it' (ibid.: para. 136). From 1912 on, Jung's point in making the distinction has been more overtly linked to his objection to Freud's understanding of imagery in dreams, myths or neurotic symptoms as substitutes for something that is or was available to the senses but which is not admitted consciously. Jung is not denying that such contents exist. But there's more, he says.

Furthermore, Jung is not denying that psychic products can have both symbolic and semiotic properties; they often do. The Definition attributes such dual nature to scientific theories, for instance. Yet, in the context of his strict separation of symbol and sign, it is like saying that a checkerboard has both white and black colours. That's very different from saying that the colour grey is a combination of black and white. An example in the latter vein could be found in Julia Kristeva's idea of a dialectical relationship between the semiotic (*le sémiotique*), to do with the instinctual rhythms of the body, and the symbolic (*le symbolique*), to do with language. She provides a compound metaphor: within the poet there rises rhythm, 'this repetitive sonority, this thrusting tooth pushing upwards before being capped with the crown of language . . . the "crown" of rhythmic thrust, limiting structure . . . destroying [rhythm] to a large degree, but also bringing it to light' (Kristeva, 1980: 28). Hauke (2000: 193) suggests that Kristeva's *le sémiotique* is 'comparable to the unknown, shadowy and unconscious' that Jung called the symbolic attitude, whereas *le symbolique* refers to 'the collective, cultural ordering and thus what is known', corresponding to Jung's semiotic. The terminological reversal aside, it is debatable whether Kristeva and Jung had the same thing in mind when referring either to the unconscious or to language (I suspect not). Jung's justification for the semantic distinction is that different psychological processes, both fundamental and irreducible to each other, are involved when some concrete imagery functions as a symbol as opposed to when similar (even the same) imagery functions as a sign.

The formation of symbols

The grounds for viewing sign and symbol as based in different processes are argued in the chapter 'Two kinds of thinking', which opens Jung's (1952[1912]) monograph (henceforth, 'Two kinds'). Signs are a function of what he calls *directed thinking*: it is a thinking-in-words, reality-oriented, communicative in origin and often intentional, ego-directed. Symbols are generated spontaneously by *associative thinking*, which is image-based, a fantasizing or dreaming. The gist of the dichotomy is traceable to Kant's distinction of intuition versus sensibility (or conception versus perception). Jung's discussion of the two modes in 1912 extended a debate to which he had already contributed. Its major participants included Eugen Bleuler and Herbert Silberer, as well as Jung and Freud.

That intense debate is little known in psychology today. It rippled into the works of Piaget and Vygotsky, but the epicentre of their own theorizing was not the same set of issues that were debated by the psychiatrists. Contemporary developmental psychologists have embraced Vygotsky as an alternative to Piaget. Vygotsky (1986[1934]) indeed developed his theory in opposition to Piaget, but he also gave space to problematizing the concept of *autistic thinking* that Bleuler developed in a dialogue with Jung (Vygotsky doesn't review Jung's position). Like Bleuler – and indirectly Jung – Vygotsky held that speech and thought have separate evolutionary origins. However, whereas Bleuler, Jung and others in their circle laboured to separate speech-based thinking from image-based thinking, Vygotsky sought to describe their dynamic union:

> The relation of thought to word is not a thing but a process, a continual movement back and forth from thought to word and from word to thought. . . . Thought is not merely expressed in words; it comes into existence through them. Every thought tends to connect something with something else, to establish a relation between things. Every thought moves, grows and develops, fulfils a function, solves a problem.
>
> (Ibid.: 218)

Interested in developmental continuities, psychologists such as Vygotsky and Piaget did not reproduce the dichotomy expounded by the medical practitioners, who on their part seemed keen to establish discontinuities between realistic and delusional thinking.

The psychiatrists' theorizing was hardly confined to psychopathology. Presenting his concept of autistic thinking to an American audience, Bleuler (1913: 875) stressed that, whilst knowledge of this mode is necessary for understanding 'morbid formations', the 'normal Psyche' too cannot be otherwise understood:

> [Autistic laws] alone throw light upon the important, but hitherto almost ignored, inner life of the individual, upon the influences which shape the creations of the poets . . . impel the peoples in the formation of their views of custom and religion, and in their dealing with home and foreign politics.

The debate centred on fine-tuning the dichotomy. Bleuler's seminal monograph was published in German under the same title and in the same year as his highly simplified USA lecture. In the monograph, Bleuler (1951[1913]: 400) acknowledges Jung's 'Two kinds': 'What I call logical or realistic thinking was called by [Jung] *directed thinking*; what I call autistic thinking, he called *dreaming* or *fantasizing*.' He agrees with what he sees as Jung's essential points, though differs on some specific issues. Silberer similarly endorsed the dichotomy, though emphasizing some slightly different aspects of it. 'Since symbols are rooted in sensuality, it is unsatisfactory to consider them merely a transition from the apperceptive to the associative form of the thought-process. Waking thinking and dream-thinking (and whatever is analogous to it) constitute a dichotomy' (Silberer, 1951[1912]: 233). He gave particular attention to hypnagogic hallucinations so as to determine the characteristics of thought organization in variable states of consciousness. In a 1909 essay quoted by Freud in a 1914 addition to *The Interpretation of Dreams*, Silberer gave the following example. Contemplating the revision of an uneven passage in an essay before falling asleep, Silberer suddenly saw himself planing a piece of wood (Freud, 1976: 460). Silberer (1951[1912]: 216) pointed out that in the 'dreams, neuroses, autosymbolic hallucinations, and the like' of modern adults, symbols substitute something that ordinarily the person could readily grasp. Substitution appears when one is '*no longer in command* of the idea underlying it'. In early human history, as in childhood, the symbol appears as 'a substitute for ideas of which humanity has *no command as yet*' (ibid.: 217). Symbols, then, form 'either by advancing toward or by receding from the idea represented by the symbol'; but in both cases, symbol formation appears as 'a falling-short-of-the-idea, as regression to a *previous* and inadequate mental level' (ibid.: 217). Towards building up his thesis, Silberer quotes at considerable length from Jung's 'The psychology of dementia praecox' (the following extracts are Rapaport's translation). The important Jungian idea for Silberer is that the conscious mind invests attention in a complex (a cluster of emotionally toned ideations), conferring upon it clarity that is lacking in lowered states of consciousness:

> One dream picture may pertain to two different complexes of waking life, even when they are sharply distinguished in the waking state. The two complex-contents merge, at least in their symbolic form, because of the decreased sensitiveness to distinctions which prevails in dreams.
> (Jung, 1907, quoted in Silberer 1951[1912]: 220–1; cf. CW3: para. 137)

Whereas Freud's notion of dream censorship endows the dream-work with intent to conceal, Jung's explanation requires only that fragments of things seen, heard and so forth, are reshuffled into some novel combination. When 'the complexes must get along in their thinking with just a fraction of clarity' there is scope 'only for vague and symbolic expressions, which consequently lack distinction and merge easily. A specific censorship for dream thoughts (in Freud's sense) need not be postulated: The inhibition issuing from the sleep-suggestion provides the necessary explanation' (Jung, 1907, quoted in Silberer 1951[1912]: 223; cf. CW3: para. 137).

When Silberer was citing Jung's 'Dementia praecox', in 1912, Jung had already moved on to the thesis of *Symbols of Transformation*. Making a case for viewing associative thinking as separate from directed thinking, he quotes William James:

> Much of our thinking consists of trains of images suggested one by another, of a sort of spontaneous reverie of which it seems likely enough that the higher brutes should be capable. This sort of thinking leads nevertheless to rational conclusions both practical and theoretical. . . . As a rule, in this sort of irresponsible thinking, the terms which fall to be coupled together are empirical concretes, not abstractions.
>
> (James, 1890: II, 325; quoted in Jung, 1952, CW 5: para. 18)

Both James and Jung point out the spontaneous or non-deliberate ('irresponsible') nature, lack of reliance on language and synthesizing function of such thinking. But their interests diverge. To James, the point made in the excerpt is a prelude to describing human reasoning as characterized by a progressive condensation of thought through seeing relations such as similarity and contiguity. Quoting James (as reproduced above), Jung omits the point that the 'links between the terms are either "contiguity" or "similarity," and with a mixture of both these things we can hardly be very coherent' (James, 1890: II, 325). To Jung, the excerpt serves as a prelude to identifying the dissociation from reality in dreaming or fantasizing. He adds that in such thinking, where 'image piles on image, feeling on feeling', there is 'an ever-increasing tendency to shuffle things about and arrange them not as they are in reality' (Jung, 1952, CW 5: para. 19). James amplifies his own point about spontaneous associations with some examples. For instance, watching a sunset led him to contemplate solar myths. As a practitioner, Jung might ask why the specific association came to James at that moment. But as a theorist, Jung wants to know why solar myths exist in the first place – and the 1912 monograph gives a complicated explanation that would become the basis for the theory of the collective unconscious and its archetypes.

Jung now addresses the 'why' question regarding symbol formation with attention, not to *how* the mind creates fantasies, but *what for*. From the outset, his explanation competed with Freud's. In 1911 – the year when everyone had something to say on the matter, it seems – Freud published 'Formulations on the Two principles of mental functioning', which links thinking to language and to the reality principle, and links fantasizing (or phantasy) to the pleasure principle. Although this corresponds to the two modes, Freud's exposition of the two principles sidesteps the questions about the formal organization of thought patterns that were debated by Bleuler, Silberer and the 'early' Jung. The diminished importance of that particular debate in psychiatry after World War II could be gleaned from Rapaport's footnote commentaries on Silberer's essay. Rapaport comments that Silberer attributes symbol formation to lowered states of consciousness without discussing how these states relate to 'unconscious motivation, censorship, and repression' (1951: 218, n. 55). He reminds us that Freud championed the understanding of symbol formation as dependent on motivational dynamics, such as wish fulfilment. Rapaport criticizes Jung's position in 'Dementia praecox' on grounds that

> This assertion fails to indicate the source of the effectiveness of the 'sleep-suggestion.' The Freudian concept of dream-censorship was little more to begin with than the conceptualization of the source and mode of effectiveness of the 'sleep-suggestion.' Jung's attempt to explain condensation as a fusion due to lack of clarity is a more anthropomorphic and less dynamic attempt than even this original conception of dream-censorship.
>
> (Ibid.: 223, n. 75)

Freud offers a reason or purpose for the particular formation. Jung's early account posits the lack of clarity as a necessary causal mechanism accounting for the formation of symbolic imagery in dreams and similar phenomena, just as speech is necessary for saying anything. His subsequent work highlights the fact that the meaning of a dream is not causally linked to the conditions that make its production possible. From this viewpoint, Freud seems to mistake an implication of the dream for a causal factor in the unconscious. Freud endows dream-work with intent: something is prevented from entering consciousness with foreknowledge of the consequences of admitting it. In contrast, Jung's account requires only that fragments of things seen, heard, emoted, etc., coalesce into some novel combination, which upon being apprehended as a *whole* reveals something about the dreamer's situation. Much later, in a footnote to his own comment on the *Tao Te Ching* passage quoted earlier, Jung would quote Richard Wilhelm: 'The relation between meaning (tao) and reality cannot be conceived under the category of cause and effect' (1951, CW 8: para. 920, n. 5).

In Jung's use, the term *image* (or *imago*) is not a mental representation of an external object. Instead, it is a fantasy idea, which expresses 'a *condensed expression of the psychic situation as a whole*, and not merely, nor even predominantly, of unconscious contents pure and simple' (1921, CW 6: para. 745). The holistic nature of the image accounts for its complexity and non-linear relation to veridical perception. A dream is a prime example. It is 'a psychic product originating in the sleeping state without conscious motivation' (Jung, 1948a, CW 8: para. 580). Contrary to Freud's notion of the dream façade, Jung contends that a dream contains its whole meaning. Its obscurity is due to our lack of understanding: 'we are dealing with something like a text that is unintelligible . . . simply because we cannot read it. We do not have to get behind such a text, but must first learn to read it' (1934, CW 16: para. 319). We learn to read it by identifying how its elements interconnect within the whole. In its entirety, the new content has a 'numinous' quality (Jung's term) in that it is felt as revealing something important, something that is not yet figured out intellectually or is known as a matter of fact. This new object of consciousness is emancipated from whatever its various components may represent in isolation. A whole is always a part of something else, however. Even in Jungian practice, the meaning of a dream is never actually gained from its text alone. Jung instructed the analyst to figure out the epistemic function of particular symbols in the person's conscious meaning-world, which entails 'a careful and conscious illumination of the interconnected associations objectively grouped around particular images', by which he means the patient's associations in the first instance (ibid.: para. 319). The greater whole within which the dream-as-a-whole makes sense is thus the dreamer's personal history, personality and worldview.

Biases built into European languages make it difficult to avoid reducing symbols to token imagery. The Oxford English Dictionary Online (retrieved March 2006) breaks down the etymology of the word 'symbol' (from the Greek for: mark, token, ticket) into *sym* and *bolos*, to throw together. The idiom is reproduced when symbolic imagery is construed as something thrown together by the psyche in order to represent something else. In contradistinction, Victor Turner (1967: 19) defined *symbol* as 'the smallest unit of ritual which still retains the specific properties of ritual behaviour'. Based on his work with the Ndembu people of Africa, he noted that their corresponding word is etymologically derived from a phrase referring to the practice of creating a trail through the forest by slashing the vegetation so as to mark the route back from the unknown bush to known paths. 'A symbol, then, is a blaze or landmark, something that connects the unknown with the known' (ibid.: 48). Spontaneous symbolic productions, such as dreams, could be viewed as actor-less acts that likewise blaze a trail from the unknown 'back' to the known or what is knowable by means of some available language.

The fugitive dialogic in Jung's theory building

Whereas defining the symbolic dimension orbited Jung's writings, defining the dialogic can find no similar centre of gravity, but could be anchored in the work of George Herbert Mead, an American social psychologist whose most influential work, *Mind, Self, and Society*, was published posthumously. His ideas made considerable impact originally in sociology, becoming the foundation for the movement of symbolic interactionism. His best-known thesis locates the origin of the self in social acts and points to its construction by means of spoken language. A person 'enters his own experience as a self or individual . . . only by taking the attitudes of other individuals toward himself within a social environment or context of experience and behaviour in which both he and they are involved' (Mead, 1934: 138). Language creates the possibility of referring to oneself, and thus provides the human being with 'some sort of experience in which the physical organism can become an object to itself' (ibid.: 137). Amongst proponents of 'dialogical' theses in psychology it became fashionable to knock Mead, following a critique by Charles Taylor (see, e.g., Hermans and Kempen, 1993) – but their own distancing from Mead is meant to strengthen the idea that selves are products of social processes. The distance already existing between Jung and Mead increases when Mead is criticized from a postmodern standpoint.

Attention to the dialogic dimension is not exactly absent in Jung's writings but has a fugitive status. We should not be misled by his use of terms such as 'social' and 'collective'. The Definition distinguishes between social and personal symbols (1921, CW 6: paras 820–1), but on closer scrutiny the 'social' is something that is a living symbol for many members of a group in parallel, and whose source cannot be traced to any particular person (e.g. religious symbols). There is no account of a *social process* whereby such symbols are jointly constructed. Jung spoke of archetypes as the human quality of the human being, the specifically human form our activities take – but his catalogue lacks archetypes of intimacy, belonging or *communitas*. Various other instances can be found so as to indicate his resistance to notions of intersubjectivity as fundamental for 'having' a self. Jung was hardly oblivious to the intersubjective construction of meaning, but he saw it as pragmatic necessity in clinical practice. Apropos 'the individuation process with its problem of opposites', Jung (1957, CW 18: para. 1172) stressed that

> This level of insight cannot be reached without the dialectical discussion between two individuals. Here the phenomenon of transference forcibly brings about a dialogue that can only be continued if both patient and analyst acknowledge themselves as partners in a common process of approximation and differentiation.

In other words, a dialogue between analyst and patient is important for clearing away obstacles to the psyche's natural movement towards its ideal state of balanced opposites (individuation). Asked to talk about transference at the Tavistock lectures, Jung was categorical in his dismissal: transference 'has nothing to do with the cure'; transference is 'compensation for a lack of rapport between the analyst and the patient' (1935, CW 18: para. 351, 385). Trueman (2005: 61) comments that, despite the importance of empathy in psychotherapy, there is surprisingly little about it in Jung's writings: 'Why didn't Jung recognize the importance of empathy?' She attributes his neglect of the topic to certain philosophical and theoretical influences. My claim is bolder: Jung was hardly passive in what influenced him. He selectively attended to certain ideas and not to others when building his theory.

Jung ignored, overlooked or contested certain ideas that were already around in the early 1900s. At the same time that he dichotomized 'associative' and 'directed' thinking, some psychologists sought to explain the dynamic interplay of the two modes. In 1911, Wundt began publishing his ten-volume *Völkerpsychologie*, completed in 1923. Summarizing his basic thesis, Wundt (1916: 74–5) poses the question, 'Wherein consists the content of primitive thought?' and answers,

> *Two* sorts of ideas may be distinguished. The one comprises that stock of ideas which is supplied to consciousness by the direct perceptions of daily life . . . But there is also a *second* class of ideas. These do not represent things of immediate perception; briefly expressed, they originate in feeling, in emotional processes which are projected outward into the environment. . . . This world of imagination, projected from man's own emotional life into external phenomena, is what we mean by *mythological* thinking.

This is very close to Jung's view on myth (the next chapter expands). Unlike Jung, however, Wundt attributed the possibility of culture and its constituents (language, myths, custom and art) to what he called gestural communication. He did not reduce culture to communicative gestures – an idea that Jung mocked in his 1912 discussion of 'directed' thinking. In *The Language of Gestures*, published in 1900, Wundt proposed that when individuals communicate, their mental states are replicated in each other, and this leads to the formation of an interpersonal configuration that he called *Volksseele* (Danzinger, 1983). As Danziger (ibid.: 309) put it, these 'individuals now become part of a relatively permanent pattern of interaction constantly enriched through associative learning . . . Gestural communication thus leads to cultural products that have an objective existence'. Wundt's theory directly influenced Mead's thought, although Mead developed it in a different direction, and partly in a criticism of Wundt.

Valsiner and van der Veer (2000) track the 'social mind' idea before Mead to Pierre Janet and James Baldwin. Jung plays no part in the history told by Valsiner and van der Veer. He is mentioned only for his attack on Janet, Freud's antagonist ('Unfortunately, it is often the case that people believe themselves to judge psychoanalysis when they are not even able to read German,' Jung opined at a controversial 1913 lecture by Janet;

Valsiner and van der Veer, 2000: 76–7). Jung took from Janet the idea of *abbaisement du niveau mental* (the lowering of mental level in neuroses), to which he refers time and again throughout his writings. Janet's later writings (1920s) concern the social origins of mental acts, but by that time, Jung's theory was firmly set on its own trajectory. Jung's review of 'directed thinking' in the 1912 monograph culminates in a page-long quotation from Baldwin, describing how social instruction shapes intellectual development. In a nutshell,

> When the child speaks, he lays before the world his suggestion for a general or common meaning; the reception it gets confirms or refutes him. . . . His next venture is from the platform of knowledge on which the newer is more nearly convertible into the common coin of effective intercourse.
>
> (Baldwin, quoted in Jung, 1952, CW 5: para. 15)

Baldwin sums up his own argument as 'material evidence and proof of *the concurrence of social and personal judgement*'; that is, co-construction or, in his words, synnomic or dual reference (quoted ibid.: para. 15). Whilst saying that he is in agreement with Baldwin, Jung hears only the message that centuries of education forced human reason to 'develop from the subjective, individual sphere to the objective, social sphere' and so produced 'a readjustment of the human mind' to its modern intellectual capacities (ibid.: para. 17). Baldwin's point seems lost on Jung. In the end, Jung quibbles that Baldwin still places speech before thought.

His quibble echoes a wider philosophical argument, which prompted others thinkers to describe the union of the two modes in language. Jung makes a similar point in his polemics, though not in his theory. He says sardonically, 'So our directed thinking, even though we may be the loneliest thinkers in the world, is nothing but the first stirrings of a cry to our companions' that water has been found, the bear was killed, a storm approaches, or wolves prowl around the camp (ibid.: para. 14). Directed thinking is more than just signals, stresses Jung. 'Language must be taken in a wider sense than speech, for speech is only the outward flow of thoughts formulated for communication' (ibid.: para. 14). He contests the 'misunderstanding that directed thinking is after all "only a matter of words"' (ibid.: para. 14). It might seem that the stone that Jung rejected in building his theory became the cornerstone of postmodern psychology, whose exponents indeed view cognitive processes as 'a matter of words'. But what exactly Jung rejects might be a caricature painted by him. In a way, the narrative of 'Two kinds' brings up the issue so as to eliminate it from the concerns of depth psychology. The discussion of directed thinking is sandwiched between the opening statement of the problem (what is the origin of symbols) and the discussion of associative thinking, where he proposes to find the solution. He does not engage with Wundt's and Baldwin's ideas even when citing them. Those ideas imply that thinking is not just 'words' but the joint construction of meaning by means of words. Instead, Jung caricatures the implication that

> The most abstract system of philosophy is . . . nothing more than an extremely ingenious combination of natural sounds. Hence the craving of a Schopenhauer or a Nietzsche for recognition and understanding, and the despair and bitterness of their loneliness. One might expect, perhaps, that a man of genius would luxuriate in the greatness of his own thoughts . . . yet he succumbs to the more powerful impulse of the herd instinct.
>
> (Ibid.: para. 14)

The comment could be read as a jibe at the Freudian inclination to reduce the reified products of the human spirit to mere instincts. But he seems to be missing the point that culture is not the secretions of isolated monadic minds. Jung's blind spot is the relevance of the Gestalt principle: a whole such as a social group is greater than or different from the sum total of its individual parts.

Defining the dialogic

Group dynamics are not reducible to an aggregate of individuals' motivations and frustrations. This is Mead's basic premise. He defined the *social act* as 'a dynamic whole – as something going on – no part of which can be considered or understood by itself – a complex organic process implied by each individual stimulus and response in it' (Mead, 1934: 7). Within this ever-evolving whole, gestures and images acquire their symbolic function, thinking in general becomes possible, and with that arises the possibility of 'seeing' oneself as a person, i.e. as someone with particular traits, states, duties and rights: 'Our thinking always takes place by means of some sort of symbols' (ibid.: 146). Mead distinguished between symbols that denote things in the world of the senses (like Jung's 'signs') and 'significant symbols', which call into being things that don't have a referent in sensory phenomena, though this concept is not the same as Jung's 'symbols' (it is not image-based). Mead pointed out that a symbol is not essential for purposive action. We may sit down without thinking about it; 'the approach to the chair is presumably already aroused in our experience, so that the meaning is there' (ibid.: 146). But if we think about it, there must be some sort of a symbol (i.e. a representation). 'It may be the form of the chair, it may be the attitude that somebody else takes in sitting down, but it is more apt to be some language symbol that arouses this response' (ibid.: 146). Mead differentiated human language from animals' 'conversation of gestures', which he illustrated with two dogs shaping up for a fight. The gesture of each dog is a stimulus for the other, eliciting an overt response, and in this way the dogs reciprocally adjust and readjust their attitude to each other. In human communication, gestures that function as symbols call out the same response in the central nervous system of both speaker and listener. Saying or hearing the word 'dog' or 'chair' invokes an inner orientation towards these objects in both speaker and listener. Mead speculates that the human CNS inhibits immediate reactions to present stimuli by responding instead to their representations (symbols) as stimuli in their own right. This allows us to imagine what could, might or ought to be – which extends human action beyond the here-and-now.

Since 'most of our acts stretch into the world that does not yet exist', the 'unit of existence is the act, not the moment,' contended Mead (1938: 65). Human beings do more than indicate things that exist independently of naming them, such as chairs and dogs. We also respond to the words as things themselves. This calls into being things that do not exist outside their naming, such as referring to someone as the Chair of a committee or son of a bitch (my examples), which are no longer about furniture or canines. Mead submits that the mental realm exists outside the 'world that is there', for it reaches forward to future possibilities and back to consequences of past actions, yet it exists only in communicative interactions in the world that is physically here and now. Immediate perceptions are integrated in a behavioural process whereby individuals observe themselves acting in relation to other persons and objects, and are thus brought into their own field of experience as an object, a 'self'. This amends William James's (1890) distinction between the self as the knowing subject and the self as the known object with the view that the self-as-known is called into being in concrete language. Mead (1938: 479) concedes Freud's premise that there are 'more profound reasons for much of our conduct than those that appear to us to be explanations of our acts' (though he queried Freud's exclusive reference to 'thwarted sexual impulses'). But, in seeking those profound reasons, Mead points us – not to an unconscious within us – but to the social act within which we become who we are.

A problem with understanding doctrines such as Mead's as a causal-developmental explanation that puts language before thought was identified by Ernst Cassirer (among others). Like Mead, Cassirer (1946[1925]: 61) stated that 'it is language that makes [man's] existence in a *community* possible; and only in society, in relation to a "Thee," can his subjectivity assert itself as a "Me"'. Like Jung, however, Cassirer queried the primacy of speech. There is a vicious circle: speech is the 'vehicle of any world perspective' but some definite perspective must be presupposed in order to explain its linguistic expression (ibid.: 31). Placing language before thought might seem to evade the vicious circle, says Cassirer, but ultimately it 'cannot bridge the gulf between the purely denotative and the expressive function of speech. In this theory, too . . . what remains obscure is exactly that *emancipation* whereby a sound is transformed from an emotional utterance into a denotative one' (ibid.: 35). Cassirer finds 'something like a new hope of a solution' in a concept of mythical ideation' (ibid.: 31), to which we shall return later. The problem to which Cassirer offered 'mythic ideation' as a solution is not quite the same problem to which postmodern psychologists offer 'discourse' as a solution. Cassirer, Jung and Bakhtin also sought to describe the relation of the bodily lived experience to its creative expression. That 'burning issue' has expired or was never kindled in the space of problems and themes that define postmodern psychology in general and social constructionism in particular. Instead, much energy was invested in persuading that a 'Me' is possible only in relation to a 'Thee' and only through language, which therefore (the argument goes) must come before the concept of self. During the second half of the last century, this basic idea was restated from several more or less independent directions. For example, Gadamer (1976: 62–3) stated,

> We grow up, and we become acquainted with men and in the last analysis with ourselves when we learn to speak. Learning to speak does not mean learning to use a preexistent tool for designating a world already somehow familiar to us; it means acquiring a familiarity and acquaintance with the world itself and how it confronts us.

To most postmodern psychologists, the developmental dependence of self-knowledge on language (as activity) does away with the Cartesian ideal of the autonomous subject. Our embedding in the flow of communicative activities ought to dispel the 'illusion that there is something in each of us to account for our sense of identity other than the fact of our personhood in an array of persons' (Harré, 1997: 186).

That idea is vividly captured by John Shotter (1996: 294), who speaks of 'our embodied embedding in this whole flow of temporally irreversible activity' by means of utterances:

> [It is] not only their fleeting, changeable nature and enormous complexity, but also their strange *dialogical* nature; which ensures that everything we do in practice, in being a response to an other or otherness in our surroundings, inevitably relates us to them in some way.

Shotter's poetic image, inspired by his reading of Bakhtin, was originally used in support of social constructionism. Lately distancing himself from social constructionism, Shotter turns to Merleau-Ponty for a better articulation of our embodied embedding (conference papers since 2000; also see O'Connor and Hallam, 2000). Those who 'move on' from social constructionism highlight the limitations of its more radical claims, but in general they do not dispute that human subjectivity is inextricably interlaced with the flow of action and its intersubjective construction. My position is similar.

The 'Bakhtin connection' is relevant here. Comparing Bakhtin and Jung from her viewpoint as a literary scholar, Susan Rowland (2005) identifies an important difference between them. Bakhtin presents 'a far more materialistic conception of social interaction . . . a constant battle between centralizing energies that aim to standardize meaning and linguistic form, versus centrifugal forces of dispersion and difference as language is embodied in actual social situations' (ibid.: 101–2). This materiality is probably why Bakhtin appeals to postmodern social psychologists. The very word *dialogue* has the immediate reference to a language-based interpersonal interaction. With or without citations of Bakhtin, the vocabulary of 'dialogue' enabled social psychologists to continue to analyse interpersonal interactions, on the one hand, whilst introducing a new perspective on the intersubjective dynamics of the construction of meaning, on the other (e.g. Marková and Foppa, 1990). Psychologists' dialogical-self theses are not a spin-off from Bakhtin's dialogism even when they find inspiration in his work (more on that in Chapter 4). Rather, what he says about utterances, they say about the self. When Shotter talks of our embodied embedding by means of utterances, his vision seems owed more to Mead than to Bakhtin. Bakhtin's dialogism fits well with a worldview that has long been familiar in the social sciences (see Holquist, 2002, on Bakhtin and Mead), but it is important to keep in mind his own context. In 'The problem of speech genres', Bakhtin (1986: 71) defines an utterance as anything from a 'short (single-word) rejoinder in everyday dialogue to the large novel or scientific treatise'. Contending with linguistics, he challenges the view of language as a static closed system, composed of sentences, which in turn are composed of words composed of syllables and phonemes. Such description studies language as separate from its communicative function. To rectify matters, he posits *utterance* as an analytic unit that is definable – not by its formal properties – but by its function as a unit of speech communication:

> The boundaries of each concrete utterance as a unit of speech communication are determined by *a change of speaking subjects*, that is, a change of speakers. Any utterance . . . has, so to speak, an absolute beginning and an absolute end: its beginning is preceded by the utterances of others, and its end is followed by the responsive utterances of others . . .
>
> (Ibid.: 71)

His talk of dialogue is both literal and a metaphor for shifts of consciousness in readers' interaction with a literary (or any) text. 'The event of the life of the text, that is, its true essence, always develops *on the boundary between two consciousnesses*' (ibid.: 106). The two consciousnesses in that instance would not be two people (writer and reader), but the reader's ordinary view and the view that she reads into the text – and which may or may not correspond to its writer's actual view. In a way, the reader becomes the author (says Bakhtin). When someone 'perceives and understands the meaning (the language meaning) of speech, he simultaneously takes an active, responsive attitude toward it. He either agrees or disagrees with it' (ibid.: 68). Shotter (1998: 39) quotes this line from Bakhtin so as to build up his own argument about 'people's unavoidable, responsive, bodily embedding in their surroundings'. It is *our* embedding as 'selves' *by means of* utterances, not the embedding of the utterances as such, to which Shotter points.

Like most fashionable jargon, the vocabulary of the dialogical could be over-stretched. My use in talking about the dialogic dimension narrows it; but I don't want to hijack the word. Bakhtin coined the word *heteroglossia* to indicate the contingency of meaning: the same word could have different meanings when uttered under different sets of conditions that are specific to the time and place. The glossary compiled by Bakhtin's translators defines *dialogism* as 'the characteristic epistemological mode of a word dominated by heteroglossia. Everything means, is understood, as a part of a greater whole – there is a constant interaction between meanings, all of which have the potential of conditioning others' (Emerson and Holquist, in Bakhtin, 1981: 426). This 'dialogic imperative, mandated by the pre-existence of the language world relative to any of its current inhabitants, insures that there can be no actual monologue' (ibid.: 426). When the self is already understood as an inhabitant of the language world, citing Bakhtin embellishes the point that there can be no 'I' apart from its multiple relations to 'you' or 'other(s)', who also inhabit language.

It is sometimes said that Jung was a dialogical thinker. Rowland (2005: 104) points out that 'most basic to Jung's position, as opposed to its conservative social colouring, is his sense of the psyche's dimension of the unknown, and its crucial role in all knowledge making'; this is what she calls 'the *dialogical* aspect of the psyche'. Her statement is firmly based in Jung's work – the dialogue analogy of the transcendent function, supplied by Jung himself, may be recalled. But to a postmodern psychologist, the phrase 'dialogical psyche' (Rowland's) sounds like the 'dialogical self' in theories discussed later in this chapter and in Chapter 4. In those, a central premise is that the many voices of one's self are internalized reflections of actual social relationships. Such an idea is alien to Jung's position, even in its superficial social colouring. The heteroglossic mismatch in the meaning of the word 'dialogical' is not a conflict about how to understand what Jung or Bakhtin were saying (at least not between Rowland and me). But the choice of words does matter. The anthropomorphic metaphor of a conversation between known and unknown parts of the psyche resonates with the postmodern discourse of discourses, and insinuates that Jung speaks 'our' language. In so doing, we lose sight of the meaning that he tried to capture by means of the analogy of imaginary numbers and the references to Zen and Buddhism (and I added Taoism). To converse or have a dialogue with the nothing-therein would be like listening to the sound of one hand clapping. If trying to define the symbolic dimension invokes the sound of one hand clapping, defining the dialogic invites the image of a handshake.

Seeing the dialogic dimension: 'being Emily'

It may be apt at this point to put a 'human face' on verbose phrases such as our embodied embedding in the irreversible flow of discourse, before continuing with high theory. This section reports a research interview involving ten-year-old Emily, Tina and Sue (not their real names), highlighting the micro-dynamics of the conversation as a social act in Mead's sense. The focus is on how Emily negotiates her positioning – hence, her experience of self – within the conversational flow. The interview was conducted in the children's school by two undergraduate students, Serena Garratt and Siân Owen. The material is used here with permission, and my analysis does not replicate theirs. They were interested in quantitative differences in aggressive and other themes generated by boys versus girls and by children with versus without behaviour problems. The schoolteacher selected nineteen same-sex groups of three, so that each group included someone with behaviour problems. The designation to the 'problem' category was based on the teacher's judgement, and was made known to the researchers only after the interviews were completed. They asked the children to imagine dream and nightmare schools. Since children inevitably use their practical knowledge of school in making up stories about imaginary schools, their criteria for what makes a school good or bad might tell us something about their real-life expectations (Jones, 1995). When planning the fieldwork, Owen and Garratt were concerned that audiotaping the interviews might make it difficult to tell who says what, which could jeopardize their hypothesis testing. So they videotaped the interviews – and some of the interviewees performed for the camera (some suspected that they were going to be on television).

The three girls sat in a line of chairs close together, facing the interviewer: Emily in the middle, Tina to her left and Sue to her right. The camera, operated by the other researcher, was behind the interviewer. It captured a wide range to either side, but it must have seemed to Tina that she was left out. Right from the start, she nudged over to Emily's chair. Throughout the interview, which lasted 14 minutes and 45 seconds, Tina kept glancing at the camera with airs of expectancy and excitement. Within six minutes, she vacated her own chair and was sitting entirely on Emily's. Sue remained sitting placidly, but being plump she pressed against Emily from the other side. Emily sat squeezed in the middle. The interview started with the interviewer asking the girls to describe the dream school, to which Tina immediately said that she would 'have a party every day'. The interviewer echoed with rising intonation, expectantly, 'A party every day, yeah?' Emily said that she would like 'a disco every day'. But she was chewing gum and her words were muffled. The interviewer echoed with lowered intonation, 'A disco and . . . [indistinct]'. Sue offered, 'A swimming pool on a beach?' The interviewer echoed this emphatically, 'A swimming pool on a *beach*? Yeah, that will be good. What else you'd have?' This set a pattern for the interview. Throughout, the girls continue to list various characteristics of the imaginary school, addressing the interviewer. She echoes and prompts for more. The girls elaborate each other's ideas, bring in new ideas, and occasionally insert a statement of what they personally like or dislike. For example, describing the nightmare school later on:

Tina   (*pulling her chair forward, though already seated on Emily's, and leaning forward so that Emily has to lean back*): It'd be a spooky creepy school (*smiles at the camera*).
Sue: And they'll be all fights and blood all dripping.

The interviewer prompts for more ideas.

Sue: Loads of swearing.
Tina: Loads of swearing too.

The other two simultaneously say something (indecipherable). Tina rocks back and forth in front of Emily, and for a moment we cannot see Emily's face.

Sue   (*to Emily*): Yeah. I hate swearing.
Emily   (*to Sue, matter-of-fact*): Oh I love it.

When reading or watching the full interview, Emily's provocative disclosure at this stage does not come as a surprise.

All the departures from the pattern established at the outset were initiated by Emily. She would interject personal stories or place herself in the fantasy in provocative ways. Michael Bamberg (2006) draws attention to what he calls 'small stories' that people insert into a conversation, which are not usually regarded as stories, and through which people fine-tune their positioning. Emily's first small story comes three minutes into the interview. Tina has just suggested that they could pick their own teacher in the dream school, and Sue amplified, 'A nice kind one'. Emily becomes animated for the first time. She announces that she likes Mrs K, who used to be their teacher but not any more. She goes on to tell about another teacher, Mr J, who had to be hospitalized. Tina joins in, speaking over

Emily's story, and presently takes over the story, recalling the glittery pop-up card that they made Mr J. Emily falls silent. The interviewer cuts in, addressing the group, 'So what about in your pretend school? What is the teacher going to be like?'

Emily   (lips moving as if answering inaudibly)
Sue: Really kind. Will let us do anything.

Emily tries to get back to telling about Mrs K, but doesn't manage to complete a sentence, because Tina and Sue also speak and the interviewer is responding to them. Presently Tina mischievously offers 'fights' (in the dream school), and Emily says almost instantly (about the hypothetical teacher):

Emily: Let us fight. I'd beat up my brother at the disco.

The interviewer echoes this questionably, and Tina – not Emily – nods vigorously. The interviewer stirs them away from the provocative theme: 'So what would the school look like?' Emily says loudly, gesturing with large arm movements, 'All lights all around the school.' Her gesturing could be viewed as an attempt physically to open room for herself, and the 'all lights' seems to connect to the disco theme, her first contribution. Emily briefly leads the exchange, but the theme is soon exhausted. When the interviewer prompts with a question about the dream-school playground, Emily becomes animated again. She suggests that they would be allowed to ride their bikes on the grass, which is forbidden in reality. She recalls a real incident, and again the other girls hijack her story by finishing it. Again, the interviewer steers them away from reminiscence by asking what else they would do in the dream classroom.

Introducing the theory of positioning, Davies and Harré (1990) point to the way in which people's contradictory storylines about what is going on are intermeshed in an unfolding conversation. In the present case, the interviewer was anxious to collect 'useable' responses, having set out to collect children's ideas about imaginary schools, and she negotiated the interviewees' recourses to real-life anecdotes and disclosures with steering prompts. This was her strategy also in the other interviews. Here, however, all slides to realism were initiated by Emily, who seemed determined to tell about herself and her world – to place an autobiographical 'I' in the jointly constructed fantasy – and the interviewer's interventions marginalized her small stories, cutting her out. Tina again was the first to respond to the question about the dream classroom:

Tina: Watching telly.
Emily: Tidying up. I wish we could tidy up.

Interviewer:	(*inaudible query to Emily*).
Emily:	Yeah I do. Me and Charlotte like to (*unclear, could be describing something she and Charlotte did*).
Interviewer:	So that's it, watch telly?
Emily:	And (*unclear*) it.
Sue:	Dance to music.
Tina	(*smiling broadly, seated on Emily's seat but pulling her own chair so to close the gap with Emily's*): Wreck everything.
Interviewer:	Wreck everything?
Emily:	Ah yes. I wish we could watch TV make a mess. Eat everything. Put Top of the Pops on. Eat everything have all drinks.

The girls now tell each other their favourite food. Just as Emily starts to say something, the interviewer cuts in, prompting for 'anything else' that they would like to have in the dream school.

Sue and Tina:	(*speaking simultaneously, indecipherable*)
Emily:	Do punching and fighting. Kick.
Interviewer:	What? You'd fight each other in your ideal school would you?
Emily and Tina:	Yeah!
Interviewer:	What else?
Sue	(*looking away at something happening off-screen*): Come into school and don't have to pay for dinner.
Emily:	(*points in the direction of Sue's gaze, says something inaudible, giggling*)
Sue	(*to Interviewer*): You could do your own printing.
Interviewer:	Do your own printing. Yeah?
Emily:	Mess up the library.
Interviewer:	You'd like to mess up the library? I thought you liked to tidy up.
Sue:	Oh yeah, doing the decorations on the Christmas tree.
Emily:	Being the cleaner (*laughs loudly*).
Interviewer:	That's what you'd like to be?
Emily:	Yeah.
Sue:	(*mutters something to Emily*).
Emily	(*to Sue*): I do at home (*folding her arms*).
Sue	(*to Emily*): How much do you clean?

The interviewer puts a stop to their private chat by introducing the nightmare school. A small story seems embedded in the above: Emily will mess up the library and then be the cleaner. In this way, via the dramatic 'punching, fighting and kicking' that momentarily got the interviewer's attention, Emily gets back to her liking of tidying up, which was initially ignored. The dark side of her 'being the cleaner' small story is not the reference to disorderly behaviour. On the contrary, it is the allusion to order. She will mess up the library and then be the cleaner. As the school cleaner, she would have adult powers. Children can only cause disorder; if they are orderly, they are merely compliant. But an adult has the power to put things right. What is Emily trying to put right?

She was the 'problem' child assigned to this group. When I first read the transcript (before seeing the video) and mentioned to the class teacher how she seems to control the conversation through subversive interjections, he said that it was typical of her. Emily positions herself as tough – she loves swearing and fighting – but on the video she doesn't come across as aggressive or hostile. Her provocative interjections are spoken calmly, in good humour. She did not react directly to Tina's invasion of her personal space, but sat squeezed in her own seat, mostly with folded arms or her hands clasped in her lap, looking straight ahead at the interviewer and calmly making outrageous statements. Her verbal aggression transpires as a non-aggressive attempt to manage an 'identity-threatening' situation without confrontation. In the power dynamics of the many-sided inter-action, her manoeuvres take on the implication of a 'look at me, I'm still here!' cry. It almost doesn't matter what she says, as long as it keeps her visible. This function of her small stories and provocative statements can come to light only when we consider them in relation to all other elements, verbal and non-verbal, of the ongoing event – a dynamic whole, no part of which can be understood on its own (cf. Mead). She is 'being Emily' by virtue of her embodied embedding in an irreversible flow of the interview – and her reactions are typical of her insofar as she uses similar self-positioning strategies in other conversational exchanges. Do we need to assume that there is something else 'behind' her positioning strategies?

Social constructionists say no. People ordinarily manage their identities in everyday conversational exchanges as spontaneously as did Emily and her peers in the interview, despite its artificiality. Positioning theory – developed by Harré and various co-writers in journal articles during the 1990s (also see Harré and van Langenhove, 1999) – invites us to understand the self as a becoming in small measure, in the immediate and mundane. Moment by moment, the person one is would be affirmed or challenged with family at home, strangers on a bus, colleagues at work . . . Positioning theory is a powerful tool. It provides a way of questioning that I applied implicitly in interpreting Emily's conduct. The theory extends Mead's via its development in Goffman's social role theory, and with poststructuralist and feminist influences. It reinforces the view that selves exist solely in conver-sational exchanges:

> According to the immanentist point of view there are only actual
> conversions, past and present. Similarities between various conversa-
> tions are to be explained by reference only to whatever concretely has
> happened before, and to human memories of it, which form both the
> personal and cultural resources for speakers to draw upon in
> constructing the present moment.
>
> (Davies and Harré, 1990: 44)

There is no self-monitoring ego behind 'the fleeting panorama of Meadian
"me's" conjured up in the course of conversational interactions,' say Davies
and Harré (ibid.: 47). They offer *position* as the 'immanentist replacement
for a clutch of transcendentalist concepts like "role"' in Goffman's formulation, which assumes supra-individual structures in society (ibid.: 44).
Roles are sets of rights and responsibilities within which our selfhood is
defined. Despite Goffman's caveats to the contrary, his dramaturgical
model invokes the objectionable dualism of actor and role. In addition,
Davies and Harré extrapolate from the theory of speech acts in linguistics
the idea that utterances are actions executing intentions. Speaking a request,
promise, or insult *performs* the request, promise or insult. Likewise, saying
'I . . .' performs personal agency. Whereas speech acts theorists, such as
John Searle and John Austin, understand the speech act as transmitting
the speaker's intention to the listener, Davies and Harré contend that 'on
the contrary, a conversation unfolds through the joint action of all the
participants as they make (or attempt to make) their own and each other's
actions socially determinable' (ibid.: 45). For instance, 'positioned as
dependent, one's cry of pain is hearable as a plea for help. But positioned as
dominant, a similar cry can be heard as protest or even reprimand' (Harré
and van Langenhove, 1991: 396). The person whose cry is interpreted as a
plea for help experiences what it means to be dependent, whilst the one
whose cry is interpreted as protest or reprimand learns what it means to be
dominant. As seen in Emily's case, the same utterances could be heard
differently when she is positioned as a 'problem' in school as opposed to
being positioned as marginalized in the interview.

It could be argued that in order for people in conversation to negotiate
their own and each other's positioning, they must somehow intuit whether
particular positions apply to them (Jones, 1997, 1999). This implicates an 'I'
that monitors the 'me' disclosed in my conversational exchanges – precisely
the notion of ego that Harré adamantly eschews. This tension intensifies in
attempts to reconcile social constructionism with the necessity of assuming
some sort of 'inner' processes. Tan and Moghaddam (1995) amend Harré's
positioning theory with their idea of 'reflexive positioning', which they define
as an intrapersonal process that parallels the interpersonal positioning
described by Harré and co-writers. 'Reflexive positions are always emerging,
changing, and shifting, based in part on how a person's utterances are

hearable to oneself as speaker'; or, as they poetically put it, an 'endless array of dances' from which one of many positioning combinations steps out (ibid.: 391). Related to that, they propose a concept of a 'dialogical self' based on William James' distinction between the 'I' and the 'Me'. The dialogical self (in Tan and Moghaddam's characterization) is the 'I' positioning a 'me' relative to other possible 'me's'. Their postulation of a process whereby 'one intentionally or unintentionally positions oneself in unfolding personal stories told to oneself' (ibid.: 389) echoes ideas and jargon that have been widely expounded since the 1980s, most conspicuously in the context of narrative psychology. While Tan and Moghaddam's thesis could be read as attempting to rescue Harré's, it reproduces the dualism inherent in James' I/me. James insisted on making it 'perfectly clear' that the psychologist's attitude is that of 'thoroughgoing dualism. It supposes two elements, mind knowing and thing known, and treats them as irreducible. Neither gets out of itself or into the other, neither in any way *is* the other, neither *makes* the other' (1890: I, 218).

It is in Mead (whom Tan and Moghaddam ignore) that the reflexivity of I/me becomes more clearly a dynamic for self-knowledge through the mediation of spoken language:

> Here [in language] is found the basis for awareness. What the individual indicates to himself, he is aware of . . . His attributes, their stresses and strains, and affective tones, he is conscious of while he sees and hears what goes on about him. Finally, the inner conversation of significant symbols, which we call 'thought', and the flow of imagery in reverie . . . constitute a central core of what is called consciousness.
>
> (Mead, 1938: 75)

In dialogical theories based in social constructionism, a notion of an inner conversation reinforces the attribution of the self to discourse whilst conceding that some conversations are imaginary. On closer scrutiny, the concession is problematic. As Vygotsky pointed out, outer speech and inner speech are 'different *functionally* (social as opposed to personal adaptation) and *structurally* (the extreme, elliptical economy of inner speech, changing the speech patterns almost beyond recognition)' (1986[1934]: 85). Although we may experience ourselves in reverie as if speaking inside our heads, the distinction between self-as-speaker and self-as-own-audience disappears. The notion of speech acts becomes inapplicable. We're back in the domain of theorizing about the (Jungian) symbolic.

'Back to the symbolic'

This chapter laboured a view of symbolic and dialogic dimensions as both fundamental to the emergence of meaning and irreducible to each other. The theories that best describe their respective implications represent antithetical perspectives on human nature. From a social constructionist standpoint, it might seem that drawing attention to the dialogic dimension eliminates the very necessity for theorizing the symbolic. From a Jungian or post-Jungian position, it might seem that the dialogic dimension pales in significance compared with the 'depth' of the symbolic. Both would be misguided. Different interests are expressed in each perspective. On the 'dialogic' side, the interest is in the unfolding of particular self-understanding within social interactions. On the 'symbolic' side, the interest is in the concrete expression of what James called the 'unshareable feeling which each one of us has . . . of his individual destiny' (1902: 499). The Jungian premise is that the unshareable feeling is expressed in symbols.

A key to Jung's theory is the notion of an actor-less act (cf. Bakhtin). This could be amplified with a reference to Cassirer. Whereas Jung, Bleuler, and others delineated two modes of thinking, Cassirer identified three: myth, language and reasoning. Myth is a 'dynamic process which produces the verbal sound out of its own inner drive' (Cassirer, 1946[1925]: 34). Like Jung, Cassirer mined the anthropological literature of the day in describing the mythic mode. He cites accounts of how 'water found by a thirsty person, a termite mound that hides and saves someone, any new object that inspired a man with sudden terror – all these are transformed directly into gods' and concludes,

> It is as though the isolated occurrence of an impression, its separation from the totality of ordinary, commonplace experience produced not only a tremendous intensification, but also the highest degree of *condensation*, and as though by virtue of this condensation the objective form of the god were created so that it veritably burst forth from the experience.
>
> (Ibid.: 33–4)

We may recall Stan's imaginary sister, who veritably burst forth when he ran to the forbidden place behind the school building (see Chapter 1). In its very formation, before any interpretation takes place, the mythic production reveals a subjective situation. In the realm of mythic conception, says Cassirer, there is 'no "reference" and "meaning" . . . thought does not confront its data in an attitude of free contemplation, seeking to understand their structure and their systematic connections . . . but is simply captivated by a total impression' (ibid.: 57).

However, a moment of captivation by total impression would not suffice for meaning to emerge. To have a meaning, the image must somehow be connected 'back' to the known realm. To have a meaning, it must acquire a reference within an already established system of statements, within which its meaning is called into being, is affirmed or challenged. It is within dialogic flows that the actor-less act acquires an actor, a reference point 'in' someone. A dream is *someone*'s dream. To have a meaning, the dream must be inserted in some narrative that seeks to understand its elements' structure and their systematic connections. The 'raw facts' of the dream acquire a meaning when narrative links are forged between those and the dreamer's wakeful circumstances. In a way, one creates a story that links dream and dreamer (who might be oneself), and in this way makes sense of its spontaneous 'bursting forth' from experience. In arriving at such a story, another creative act is performed – an act that is characterized by its own uniqueness as an actual and effective performance. For this new act to be meaningful, it must be nested in yet another narrative (e.g. justifying a particular interpretation of the dream by reference to some theoretical framework, such as Jungian or Freudian). The next chapter picks up more or less from this point.

Chapter 3

Myth and narrative

For years I have been observing and investigating the products of the unconscious in the widest sense of the word, namely dreams, fantasies, visions, and delusions of the insane. I have not been able to avoid recognizing certain regularities, that is, *types* . . . that repeat themselves frequently and have a corresponding meaning.

(Jung, 1951, CW 9I: para. 309)

It is an unfortunate misunderstanding (a legacy of rationalism) to think that the truth can only be the truth that is composed of universal moments; that the truth of a situation is precisely that which is repeatable and constant in it. . . . the question is whether this unity will really be a fundamental and essential unity of Being . . . not unity, but *uniqueness*, the uniqueness of a whole that does not repeat itself anywhere and the actuality of that whole.

(Bakhtin, 1993: 37)

Concluding his discussion of associative thinking in the 1952 (1912) monograph, Jung analyses a piece by Anatole France (my thanks to Terence Dawson for translating that piece). It is an anecdote about Abbé Oegger, the first dean of the cathedral of Paris, who was troubled by the question of whether Judas was damned and eventually concluded that Judas was redeemed. Jung makes two general points. One point is that the recurrence of mythic motifs is due to their signification of a typical human situation. 'The Judas legend is itself a typical motif, namely that of the mischievous betrayal of the hero'; this 'myth is moving and tragic, because the noble hero is not felled in fair fight, but through treachery' (1952, CW 5: para. 42). The motif thus expresses a constellation of emotions, motivations and actions, which repeatedly appears in history and fiction. He notes that, as a general rule, the 'mythological tradition . . . does not perpetuate accounts of ordinary everyday events in the past, but only of those which express the universal and ever-renewed thoughts of mankind' (ibid.: para. 42). His other point is that the 'mechanism of fantasies in general' involves a conscious organization of unconscious material: conscious fantasies 'illustrate, through the use of mythological material, certain tendencies in the personality which are not yet recognized or are recognized no longer' (ibid.: paras 44–5). The priest's doubts and hopes concerning Judas 'in reality revolve around his own personality, which was seeking a way to freedom through the solution of the Judas problem' (ibid.: para. 44). In reality, Jung is analysing a character in a story (even if based on someone who once lived). If it were an autobiographical account by the real Oegger, it might be of interest to narrative psychologists; but Jung's analysis would still be at odds with the ethos of narrative analysis. His analysis of the anecdote lacks attention to how the text communicates certain meanings through its structural, stylistic and linguistic aspects. Jung sees in literature simply further evidence that 'the human psyche is the womb of all the arts and sciences' (1950, CW 15: para. 133). This is consistent with his approach to dreams, though with a caveat. In literature, 'we are confronted with a product of complicated psychic activities – but a product that is apparently intentional and consciously shaped' (ibid.: para. 134). In contrast, the sole source of dreams is 'obviously autonomous psychic complexes which form themselves out of their own material' (1948a, CW 8: para. 580).

Jung wanted to get as near as possible to the 'raw' organizing process. He turns from the Abbé Oegger story to a series of fantasies that he believed 'owe their existence . . . to the exclusive activity of the unconscious' (1952, CW 5: para. 46). The series was written by Miss Frank Miller, which Jung assumed was a pseudonym for a patient of Théodore Flournoy (who published the material in 1906). Unbeknown to Jung it was her real name, and she wrote the fantasies to help Flournoy with his publication (Bair, 2003). It is an open question whether the historical fact undermines the general theory that Jung based on his analyses of Miss Miller's literary fantasies. Probably not; his theory is problematic for other reasons.

Between 1919 and 1921, young Bakhtin was writing *Toward a Philosophy of the Act* (posthumously published and translated in 1993), where he argued spiritedly that it is an unfortunate misunderstanding to think that the truth is the repeatable and constant element in separate situations. Also between 1919 and 1921, Jung, entering his maturity in years and as a theorist, hit upon the terminology of archetypes. Although the theory is already present in the 1912 publication of *The Psychology of the Unconscious*, the term seems to be first used in 'Instinct and the unconscious' in 1919 and integrated into *Psychological Types* in 1921. Archetype is not granted a listing of its own in the Definitions, but is discussed as synonymous with 'primordial image' under the entries for Image and Idea. The term was retrospectively inserted into the 1952 revision of the 1912 monograph. Jung too asked about the spontaneous, creative and unique, but his answers are a psychologist's answers. They gravitate towards the identification of the repeatable and constant. His discovery of the archetypes seems to rest on precisely the unfortunate misunderstanding exposed by Bakhtin: he recognized certain regularities that repeat themselves. Jung proceeds to list motifs 'arranged under a series of archetypes' such as the Shadow, Wise Old Man, Child, Mother, Maiden, and 'lastly the *anima* in man and the *animus* in woman' (1951, CW 9I: para. 309). The classification into types robs each one of those dreams, fantasies, etc., of the uniqueness of its actual and effective performance, with which Bakhtin was fascinated.

Jung might be wrong about some implications of the phenomena that he called archetypal, but his derivation of a repeatable and constant element in creative acts is not necessarily fallacious or a mere folly of rationalism. It concerns the question of how experiences become *organized* (hence meaningful), not merely expressed or 'let out' by means of creative acts. To Jung, the psyche is unequivocally the organizer, the nothing-therein, whence meaning emerges. In contrast, postmodern psychologists locate the organization of experience in the narrative itself. Meaning is said to emerge from *how* something is told; that is, not only what is actually said, but also from how it is structured and its other stylistic, grammatical and linguistic characteristics. Viewing narrative as the 'organizer' locates the emergence of meaning(s) in open-ended never-ending chains of iterative acts, in interpretations piled upon interpretations. During the 1980s, various convergent ideas and interests coalesced into the claim that the self is characterized by narrativity. The postmodernists redescribed the human subject as '*homo narrans* . . . a storyteller who both finds herself in stories already told and strives for a self-constitution by emplotting herself in stories in the making' (Schrag, 1997: 26). In psychology, the theme is sometimes referred to as the literary metaphor of the self. Like Jung, narrative psychologists are seldom interested in the literary as such but describe processes of selfhood. It is assumed that the narrative forms found in literature are emulated also in personal stories, which either express or effect self-understanding. Jung and others in his circle saw telltale 'effects' of intrapsychic dynamics or structures in myths.

Myth and psyche

'No three blind men ever investigated the essential nature of the elephant with more surprising results than those who have sought the single answer which would unlock the mystery of the origin and nature of tales and myths,' commented the folklorist Stith Thompson (1955: 178). Jung's answer is surprising indeed. Myths are manifestations of archetypes; and an archetype 'might suitably be described as the instinct's perception of itself' (1948b, CW 8: para. 277). The animal that Jung sees in the proverbial elephant is unique in some respects, but in other respects coincides with others' answers (notably with Lévi-Strauss: Gras, 1981). For the present purposes, suffice it to locate Jung's view in a roughly sketched array of approaches to myth.

Phillip Wheelwright (1955) noted a polarization of viewpoints. On the one side, there are theories concerning 'primary myth' in that they refer to 'a basis, and even perhaps in some instances as a pre-linguistic tendency, of human envisagement' (ibid.: 155). On the other, there are theories concerning 'romantic myth', which connotes '*le roman*, or deliberately contrived story' (ibid.: 156). On the primary-myth side, Cassirer treats myth as 'a synonym of the mythopoeic mode of consciousness' (ibid.: 154). This is echoed in Lévy-Bruhl's theory of *participation mystique* and in Susanne Langer's treatment of myth as a primary mode of human expression that is parallel to, but not the same as, language and art (ibid.: 155). They define myth 'without any necessary implication of "narrative" (although recognizing that mythic envisagement may . . . have a strong tendency to develop into narrative forms)' (ibid.: 155). Wheelwright finds the extreme opposite view in Richard Chase's *Quest for Myth*, published in 1949. Chase viewed the earliest mythmakers as 'individual poets . . . constructing out of their especially sensitive imaginations tall tales characterized by a peculiar complication of "brilliant excitement, of the terrific play of the forces natural and human"' (ibid.: 155). Chase claimed, 'myth is literature and must be considered as an aesthetic creation of the human imagination' (quoted ibid.: 155). Wheelwright concludes, 'It is pretty obvious that Chase, who takes myth as a species of literature, and Langer, who follows Cassirer in distinguishing between myth and art as separate categories, are not working from the same initial definition' (ibid.: 155). Wheelwright brings the poles together in what he calls 'consummatory myth': 'a post-romantic attempt to recapture the lost innocence of the primitive mythopoeic attitude by transcending the narrative, logical, and linguistic forms which romantic mythologizing accepts and utilizes' (ibid.: 156).

Wheelwright's 'primary versus romantic' dichotomy could be supplanted with a broader 'psychological versus literary' attitude to theorizing about myth (not necessarily reflecting what literary scholars and psychologists may do). On the literary side, there are descriptions of the diversity and poetic imagery of mythological stories. On the psychological side, there are inquiries about what the occurrence of these stories tells about the mind creating them. There is also a 'sociological' attitude, expressed in theories that link myths to group processes, instances of which are found in works by Wundt, Émile Durkheim and Bronislaw Malinowski, among others. Based on his fieldwork with the people of Trobriand in New Guinea, Malinowski describes myth as 'a vital ingredient of human civilization' (1971[1926]: 19). Myth 'is not merely a story told but a reality lived. It is not of the nature of fiction, such as we read today in a novel' (ibid.: 18). The various short accounts of a particular myth are each only a part – 'and a rather insignificant one' (ibid.: 43) – of a bigger story that is not told but lived. What really matters about the myth is its social function. Myth is 'not an idle tale, but a hard-working active force . . . not an intellectual explanation or an artistic imagery, but a pragmatic charter of primitive faith and moral wisdom' (ibid.: 19).

Malinowski's view accommodates both the literary and psychological attitudes. He points out that, while myth is 'above all a cultural force', it is 'obviously also a narrative, and thus has its literary aspect' (ibid.: 87). The more dramatic myths, especially of death and the spirit world, seem to reflect deep psychological states. With the 'vivid texture of their myths, stories and beliefs', the people of Trobriand 'would screen . . . the vast emotional void gaping beyond them' (ibid.: 78). The already fuzzy boundaries between literary, psychological and sociological attitudes to theorizing about myth become further blurred in postmodernism. Both Jung and Malinowski are 'modern'; they approach actual myths as empirical phenomena in need of classification and explanation. Postmodernist approaches understand myth as fundamentally narrative. Unlike what Wheelwright called 'romantic myth', the postmodernist construes narrative itself as a primary mode of conception. Related to that, myth is understood as a form of speech that embodies an ideology – it is thus a reality lived – and not confined to the imaginative productions of ancient or aboriginal mythologies (e.g. Barthes, 1993[1957]).

Bruce Lincoln (1999) – whose adage is *myth is ideology in narrative form* – provides an exceptionally illuminating account of myth theories from the Ancient Greeks through to modernity. The most relevant in the present context is the Central European tradition of comparative mythology and the related paradigm of land-myth-and-*Volk*, traceable to Herder in the late eighteenth century. This tradition persists in Jung, according to Lincoln. He lists Jung along with numerous others without reviewing his theory (the links made below are mine). Herder is generally accredited with the modern meaning of culture that informs postmodern psychology. He distinguished between 'social relations that are based merely on power or contract' and *Volk* as 'a primary cultural community', where social relations 'enter into the very formation of individual personality' (Danziger, 1983: 303). Early nineteenth-century German romanticism transformed Herder's emphasis on temporal and developmental aspects of culture into 'a one-sided emphasis on the past and an opposition to all further development' (ibid.: 304). Danziger notes that a nineteenth-century account of the relationship between individual and culture, based on the psychologizing of culture, received its twentieth-century 'incarnation and most radical form' in the theories of Jung and Freud (ibid.: 306).

Back to myth: Lincoln summarizes Herder's thesis as follows. Myths are 'part of the fall from primordial human unity' and 'a treasured possession of each *Volk*, without which its identity and continuity would be quite impossible' (Lincoln, 1999: 54). Myth is a discourse of differentiation, for *Völker* develop through their distinctive stories. Scholars adopting that view could either describe the diversity of myths, 'showing how idiosyncratic narrative details correspond to the values, character, climate and experience distinctive of the *Volk* who tell them' (ibid.: 54). Or they could focus on issues of unity, 'using the evidence of myths to trace the world *Völker* back to their place of common origin' (ibid.: 54). Herder thought of that place geographically, and believed to have pinpointed it to a location in Central Asia. Jung picks up the gist with an important twist: he looks to biology, and believes he has found the site of primordial unity in the psyche.

Herder and Jung are separated by more than a century of intense debates and intensive theorizing about myth, unfolding against the wider backdrop of political and social changes. Lincoln notes that nineteenth-century scholars, such as Durkheim and Mauss, transferred a Darwinian model of evolution from the biological to the cultural sphere, orienting their professional mission towards the category of the 'primitive'. Identifying myths as the stories of primitive peoples, the 'pioneer anthropologists' described certain themes as 'irrationalities that revealed the childhood of human thought' (ibid.: 70). In Lincoln's account, their perspective reflected and legitimated the late nineteenth-century burst of colonial expansion by supplying a narrative in which the 'savages' lacked, 'not the Christian gospel, but reason and/or history' (ibid.: 70). Jung connects to that narrative obliquely. He endorses it by accepting implicitly the category of the primitives and the isomorphism of childhood and the evolution of consciousness. Yet he subverts the colonial thrust by finding the irrationalities of the prehistoric primitive still alive in the soul of the modern European adult beneath the cumulative layers of history and civilization. Lincoln sums up:

> Following the trajectory that began with Herder, leading figures of romanticism were glad to embrace myth. They did so as part of their rejection of Enlightenment values, but also found it useful to yoke this newly lionized category to *völkisch* and nationalist projects. . . . This orientation takes for granted that nations, 'cultures', and/or *Völker* . . . are primordial, bounded, unproblematic entities and that myth is the equally primordial voice, essence, and heritage of the group. Myth and group are understood to be linked in a symbiotic relation of co-reproduction, each one being simultaneously producer and product of the other.
>
> (Ibid.: 210)

Jung's distinctive application of myth to psychology embodies an understanding of myth and psyche (rather than myth and group) as linked in the symbiotic relation of co-reproduction. Jung attributes *völkisch* and nationalist projects to the archetypal configuration of the psyche. For instance, 'mother country' and 'fatherland' are allegories of mother and father, yet their 'power to stir us does not derive from the allegory, but from the symbolical value of our native land' (1922, CW 15: para. 128). Such analogies tap into the archetype of 'the *participation mystique* of primitive man with the soil on which he dwells, and which contains the spirits of his ancestors' (ibid.: para. 128). Whether he misunderstood the anthropological studies of the day or chose to reinterpret the evidence, Jung believed that culture rests on inherited dispositions. 'The collective unconscious contains the whole spiritual heritage of mankind's evolution, born anew in the brain structure of every individual' (Jung, 1931b, CW 8: para. 342). In sharp contrast, Durkheim and Mauss (1963[1903]) spoke of a 'collective mind' as an emergent property of joint activities. They saw primitive classifications and mythologies emerging from tribal communities' awareness of their own social organization, and saw the weakening hold of religion as making room for scientific reasoning. Jung sees hereditary residues of ancestral experiences in all spheres of culture – religion, science, ethics and art – and regards the developments in those as 'variants of archetypal ideas, created by consciously applying and adapting those ideas to reality' (1931b, CW 8: para. 342).

Studying Jung as a myth theorist, Robert Segal (1999) proposes that Jung articulated an understanding that was new at the time: myth as being about the mind, not about the world. It could be argued that since psychology was anyway about the mind, and Jung was a psychologist, he set out to describe the psyche rather than to explain myth (Jones, 2003c). He was not alone in that particular respect. Bair (2003) describes how around 1910 the race was on amongst psychiatrists and psychoanalysts to publish about myths. Their approach to myths was subordinate to the explanation of dreams and delusions. Jung viewed mythological motifs, including those appearing in types of fantasy that are not studied by myth theorists, as manifestations of archetypes. He proposed that

> There are as many archetypes as there are typical situations in life. Endless repetition has engraved these experiences into our psychic constitution, not in the form of images filled with content, but at first only as *forms without content*, representing merely the possibility of a certain type of perception and action.
>
> (1936, CW 9I: para. 99)

Quoting 'There are as many archetypes as there are typical situations in life', Segal suggests that there is an unlimited number and multiple functions of archetypes (1999: 94). His interpretation reflects a fascination with the diversity of myths and their cultural contingence. Jung took the other Herderian option, and his message to psychologists is the opposite one. To him, the diversity of myths acquires the paradoxical significance of evidence for the uniformity of the psyche. Human life anywhere, in any era, invariably oscillates between experiences of hunger and satiation, belonging and

abandonment, love and loss, empowerment and helplessness, and more –
but the number of typical situations is finite:

> Like the instincts, the primordial images have been obscured by the
> extraordinary differentiation of our thinking. Just as certain bio-
> logical views attribute only a few instincts to man, so the theory of
> cognition reduces the archetypes to a few, logically limited categories
> of understanding.
>
> (1948b, CW 8: para. 274)

In analysing myths and likewise occasionally considering literature, Jung
labours to peel off the extraordinary differentiation of our 'directed'
thinking so as to uncover the few, logically limited categories of human
understanding – categories that the faculty of knowledge seems to supply
from itself. In contrast, postmodern psychologists seek to locate human
understanding in the ongoing ever-changing flow of that extraordinary
differentiation of our meaning-worlds.

Some 'peculiarities' of Jung's scholarly style reproduce the German
tradition of his day and directly link to intellectual debates that would have
been familiar to his contemporaries. These include his frequent forays into
comparative etymology. Such forays are often yoked to subtle arguments
with *Völkerpsychologie* scholars such as Kuhn or Steinthal, names that
nowadays are confined to history and whose ideas are scarcely known (at
least in psychology). But the arcane trappings of Jung's theory should not
detract from its own effectiveness as an ideology in narrative form. The
mythic narrative 'packages a specific, contingent system of discrimination
in a particularly attractive and memorable form. What is more, it naturalizes and legitimates it' (Lincoln, 1999: 147). The Jungian narrative inherits
a certain system of discrimination that was specific to post-Herderian
thinking – e.g. the category of the primitives – but it naturalizes and
legitimates another 'active social force' that came into play in modernity. It
is the myth which Rieff (1959), focusing on Freud, dubbed 'Psychological
Man'. Focusing on Jung, Homans (1995: 5) sums up Reiff's idea: Psychological Man is 'characterized by inner diffuseness: he can organize or
structure the inner, personal, and private dimension of his experience of the
contemporary world only through psychology'. If Psychological Man is a
modern myth, its postmodern counterpart is *Homo narrans*, the human
subject who organizes and structures her experiences by means of intermeshed cultural and personal stories.

Roland Barthes (1993[1957]) defined myth as a form of speech that turns
history into nature. He notes, 'paradoxical as it may seem, *myth hides
nothing*: its function is to distort, not to make disappear' (ibid.: 121). A
myth distorts by disconnecting something from its historical becoming and
regards it instead as a manifestation of an essential order. Jungian

psychology indeed distorts social history and the historicity of the myths told by ancient and aboriginal peoples into manifestations of essential human nature. But before rushing to condemn Jung on Barthes' cue, it is worth heeding Lincoln's caveat: 'If myth is ideology in narrative form, then scholarship is myth with footnotes' (1999: 209). Barthes' footnotes on myth legitimate a new myth, according to which expositions of historicity are myth-free. Apropos of the study of autobiography in literary studies, Sprinker (1980: 324) commented that Barthes, Derrida, Lacan and others produced a 'ceaseless torrent of writing' trying to establish the primacy of a 'textual, non-subjective "I"' as the 'creator/originator/producer of a discourse'. Within a few years of his comment, variants of this textual subject entered also psychology as a new myth, a new 'ideology in narrative form'.

Narrative and the self

It seemed as if suddenly in the 1980s everyone was talking about narratives, narrative knowledge and the narrativity of the self. Almost simultaneously in anthropology, sociology, health, business, education, psychotherapy and psychology there emerged a movement sometimes called the 'narrative turn', sometimes the 'interpretative turn' (Polkinghorne, 1989). A corresponding interest in autobiography appeared slightly earlier in literary studies (e.g. Olney, 1980). The anthropologist Marianne Gullestad (1996) links the academic interest to the rise in 'popular' consumption of autobiographies and biographies. Accelerated changes and fragmentation of present-day society turned identity and self-creation into crucial issues. Due to globalization, many people have become sceptical about the possibility of knowledge that is not situated in particular contexts. When the 'grand' narratives of science and politics lose their power, '"little" narratives, such as autobiography, gain credibility. An autobiography has the advantage of being clearly positioned: one person is locating him or herself in the world' (ibid.: 17).

The sociologist Anthony Giddens (1991) described the consequences of late modernity for experiencing oneself. In traditional societies, life transitions were staked out against the backdrop of a relatively unchanging social order. In modern societies, 'the altered self has to be explored and constructed as part of a reflexive process of connecting personal and social change' (ibid.: 33). Such self-management requires the regularized use of abstract knowledge, which in turn depends directly or indirectly on literacy. Literacy makes it possible to abstract systems of knowledge and to examine them in terms of intelligibility rather than past performance. We live 'a biography reflexively organized in terms of flows of social and psychological information about possible ways of life' (ibid.: 14). Consequently, self-identities are formed 'in the capacity *to keep a particular narrative going*' (ibid.: 54). The psychologist Dan McAdams (1999: 487) quotes this line so as to amplify his own position on narrative identity, based more directly on psychodynamic theory, which he began putting forward in the mid-1980s.

Generally in psychology, the interest in personal stories is arrived at from diverse and sometime conflicting meta-theoretical positions. At the radical extreme, passionate pleas were initially made for a clean break with the past. The new psychology would 'liberate the telling', challenge the 'master myth of current psychological science', which allows only one voice and privileges the 'experimental story', and would make psychology 'more clearly' literature and advocacy (Mair, 1988: 133). It was claimed that everything that psychologists study is storied or story-like ('save for that part . . . that deals with sensory physiology': Sarbin, 1986: 8). At the conservative end, a focus on narrative is smoothly assimilated into 'traditional' psychologies, though invigorated with contemporary sensitivities. Two decades on, narrativism has not usurped the 'master myth' of mainstream psychology. Instead, there emerged a robust multidisciplinary research field that generates its own concerns and momentum, into which some psychologists are drawn. It may be helpful to think of auto/biography studies as a late-twentieth-century academic pursuit that cuts across the disciplinary divisions that were inherited from the late nineteenth century, and to view 'narrative psychology' as the enfolding of that pursuit in a particular corner of the academia. Although a kind of 'philosophy' informs the movement as a whole, it would be more accurately described as a form of empirical study. However, methodological issues of how best to analyse personal stories – which narrative scholars may get excited about – become irrelevant when we ask how Jung versus narrative psychologists theorize about selfhood and meaning.

Timely philosophical works published between 1984 and 1994 – the formative decade of the narrative movement – provided the preoccupations of the era with an authoritative voice. Their significance for psychology is difficult to assess. Like the borrowings from Bakhtin, citations of Alaisdair MacInytre, Charles Taylor, Paul Ricoeur and Richard Rorty embellish psychologists' own claims. Conversely, the psychologist Jerome Bruner is often cited by 'narrative' scholars in other disciplines. Yet Bruner (1986, 1990), writing for psychologists, was importing basic ideas from literary theory so as to identify 'narrative' as a cognitive mode. Coinciding with Bruner's first book on the subject, Theodore Sarbin presented a landmark edited volume, *Narrative Psychology*. In the influential essay that opens the volume, he quotes from MacIntyre's *After Virtue*:

> In successfully identifying and understanding what someone else is doing we always move towards placing a particular episode in the context of a set of narrative histories . . . It is because we all live out narratives in our lives and because we understand our own lives in

terms of the narratives that we live out that the form of narrative is appropriate for understanding the actions of others. Stories are lived before they are told – except in fiction.

(MacIntyre, 1984: 211–12; quoted in Sarbin, 1986: 11)

After Virtue does not actually build up an argument leading to the claim that we all live out narratives. Rather, it seems like common sense brought to bear on MacIntyre's thesis about ethics in the twentieth century. Taylor (1989: 47), who does theorize about the self, posits the fact that 'we grasp our lives in a *narrative*' as an 'inescapable feature of human life' and a 'basic condition of making sense of ourselves'. He expands, with footnote citations of MacIntyre and Bruner:

It has often been remarked that making sense of one's life as a story is . . . not an optional extra; that our lives exist also in this space of questions, which only a coherent narrative can answer. In order to have a sense of who we are, we must have a notion of how we have become, and of where we are going.

(Ibid.: 47)

Taylor argues persuasively that to 'have' a self requires an orientation in a space of moral questions, belonging in a community of speakers and having a narrative about one's history. However, such understanding was already around when Taylor articulated it exhaustively. It is as if a consensus was achieved about a 'theory' without a clear author.

The movement has its critics, but there is no sustained opposition matching its sweep across the academia. Mostly, scholars take it or leave it – are taken by it or remain indifferent. Some criticisms might be misplaced due to disciplinary drift. 'The idea of the self as something wholly constructed out of the narratives we create about our lives has become a staple across the humanities. But it's utter nonsense, says Galen Strawson' (*The Guardian*, 10 January 2004). He says it in a review of a recent book by Bruner (2004). As a philosopher, Strawson is concerned with the 'factual' or metaphysical question of whether there is something that could be called a self. Although Bruner concurs with the narrativity assumption as made in the humanities in general, his own emphasis is different. For two decades he has proclaimed it from the viewpoint of a culture-oriented developmental psychologist, inspired significantly by Vygotsky. His concern is with ontogenesis more than with ontology; that is, not so much 'what' is the self, but how an understanding of oneself develops in human beings.

Although the narrative movement is characterized by blurred disciplinary boundaries, it acquired variegated colouring as it travelled across the academia. In literary studies, Worthington (1996: 13) defined the self as 'a creative narrative process achieved within a plurality of intersubjective communicative protocols'. He adds that there must be an integration of the multiple selves: 'In thinking myself . . . I draw together my multiple members – past and other subject positions – into a coherent narrative of selfhood which is more or less readable by myself and others' (ibid.: 13). More or less the same idea underpins also narrative psychology. But emphases vary. In psychology, Freeman (1997: 171) points out that the discipline's traditional categories leave out 'human lives, existing in culture and in time'. Narrative psychology fills the gap, for it is 'geared towards the experiential' and the study of people, 'not in the somewhat contrived situation of the lab or the controlled experiment . . . but in their "natural habitat" as they actually live' (ibid.: 172). Narrative psychology centres on the uniquely individual by applying hermeneutic methods that aim for interpretation and understanding. Its unit of analysis is the individual life, according to Freeman. In practice, the unit would be someone's *story* of their own life. Sceptics who maintain that psychology ought to be the 'science' of mind and behaviour may fail to see why the gap identified by Freeman requires filling. In literary studies, the 'turn' is associated with a shift from text to subject (whilst continuing to analyse texts). In psychology, the shift is from subject to text (whilst continuing to theorize about the subject). James Olney (1980: 21) pointed out that behind every literary work, and likewise autobiography, there is an '"I" informing the whole and making its presence felt at every critical point . . . coming awake to its own being shapes and determines the nature of the autobiography'. Scholars who arrive at the study of autobiography in social scientific contexts tend to have in mind a living person interacting with their own story:

> Autobiography can be read as a *dialogue* that the author keeps with himself or herself. There is a distance between the self who writes and the self who was, a distance between the now of the writing and the then of the narrated past.
>
> (Gullestad, 1996: 5)

The living person who may maintain a dialogue with herself by means of autobiography is clearly not identical with the 'I' that is latent in how the story is told. Fascinated by how a life becomes a text, Olney (1972) analysed Jung's autobiography unperturbed by the extent to which it was edited, and in some parts written, by Aneila Jaffé. Indisputably, there is an 'I' informing the whole of *Memories, Dreams, Reflections*, making its presence felt throughout, and it gives us an image of Jung. The question of who exactly wrote what would become acute if specific parts were to be analysed as a dialogue that Jung kept with himself.

Generally in the social sciences, claims about the ontology of the self often subserve empirical research questions. Medical sociologists Kelly and

Dickinson (1997: 274) state categorically: 'the sociological self *is* . . . the narratives which people use to present their autobiographies'. However, this declaration of their theoretical position is meant to defend an investigation that is not designed to 'test' the narrativity hypothesis. Kelly and Dickinson investigated how people with irritable bowel syndrome understand their illness and its implications for intimate relationships, employment and other aspects of their life. The onset of a serious illness is a biographical disruption, to which some people react with narrative reconstruction of their outlook on self and world. Saying that the analysis of personal stories is a good way of finding out how people cope with illness or trauma is not the same as saying that the self is wholly or even partially those stories, although typically empirical interests in personal narratives are closely yoked to ontological claims. In the social scientific context, narrative analysis or narratology refers to an epistemological ethos inspired by the interpretative and hermeneutic methods of the humanities. It involves 'a synthesizing of the data rather than a separation into its constituent parts' (Polkinghorne, 1995: 15). The ostensible object of investigation is the story itself: the method 'examines the informant's story and analyses how it is put together, the linguistic and cultural resources it draws on, and how it persuades a listener of authenticity' (Riessman, 1993: 2). Some psychologists who analyse personal stories – and may or may not call themselves 'narrative psychologists' – regard the person telling the story as the object of investigation. For example, investigating fear of crime, Hollway and Jefferson (2000: 32) contend that, unlike narratology, their own analysis is focused on 'the people who tell us stories about their lives: the stories themselves are a means to understand our subjects better'. Similarly, advocating a narrative approach in psychology and psychotherapy, Luis Botella and associates (1997) contend that hermeneutic methods in this context should not perform a merely stylistic, grammatical or purely linguistic analysis of texts, but should instead provide a framework for reading self-narratives in search of a better understanding of their authors' identity constructions. When psychologists and psychotherapists regard some life stories as 'better' than other stories, they hardly make judgements about literary merit, but about how well the person who tells it might be, mental health-wise. It is another way of saying that some outlooks on life are better than other outlooks in terms of coping with trauma and stress. Translating that common sense into narrativism results in the implication that one's 'story' does not have to be told aloud or even in inner speech.

The psychologizing twist of literalizing the self is that the narratives we live by need not be narrated at all. Rather, the 'narrative self' emerges as an abstract structure that is said to be 'like a text about how one is situated with respect to others and the world' (Bruner, 1986: 130). Some proponents of the narrative approach link the idea to the theory of personal constructs developed by George Kelly in the 1950s. Kelly's contention was that people are not victims of their biography, though they could be enslaved by their interpretation of it. He introduced his epistemological position with the analogy of looking at one's world 'through transparent patterns or templates which [one] creates and then attempts to fit over the realities of which the world is composed' (Kelly, 1963: 8). In their programme for the narrative approach, Botella and associates (1997) 'postmodernize' Kelly's metaphor. Paraphrasing James' I/me distinction, they propose that the self-as-author (I) constructs an 'analogue space' and observes the self-as-actor (me) moving in that space, a process that they call 'narratization'. From the viewpoint of social constructionism, ideas such as an 'analogue space' are reminiscent of Cartesian dualism. 'Somehow they assume an ego whilst denying it,' opine van Langenhove and Harré (1993: 93), referring specifically to a version of the literary metaphor of the self that was proposed by Kenneth and Mary Gergen. In most of its versions, however, the *narrative self* is construed as a 'more or less coherent self (or self-image) that is constituted with a past and a future in the various stories that we and others tell about ourselves' (Gallagher, 2000: 14).

In that vein, Dan McAdams (e.g. 1985, 1993, 1999, 2001) defines self-identity as a way in which the self can be arranged or configured, and which takes the form of a story, complete with setting, scenes, character, plot and theme. His starting point is psychodynamic ego psychology, with particular reference to Erik Erikson's theory of psychosocial development. Erikson (1968: 211) defined the ego as 'a central and partially unconscious organizing agency' which, at any stage in life, must deal with a changing representation of self 'which demands to be synthesized with abandoned and anticipated selves' at the interface between self and social reality. McAdams likewise distinguishes ego from self-identity. Paraphrasing William James' I/me distinction, the ego (I) is 'the authorial process, the synthetic selfing function . . . the orienting perspective' (McAdams, 1998: 35). Narrative self-identity (me) is the result of that process. McAdams formulated a concept of *imago*, defined as 'a personified and idealized image of the self that functions as a protagonist during particular chapters of the life story' (1999: 486). His early research into life stories identified an array of such self-images – self as warrior, traveller, caregiver, lover, healer, teacher and more – which seem to fall into two broad categories, corresponding to Bakan's identification of 'agency' versus 'communion' personality orientations. Some of his more recent research is focused on the life-story plot, rather than protagonist.

Gergen (1994) suggests that storytelling conventions govern how life stories are told. Life stories may have a 'progressive' happy-ever-after plot, in which one's situation later in life is evaluated more positively than the earlier situation is, or the 'regressive' plot of a tragedy. There could be various subordinate forms, such as the heroic saga and its ups-and-downs. To Gergen, self-narratives are 'forms of social accounting or public discourse . . . conversational resources, constructions open to continuous alteration as interaction progresses' (ibid.: 188), and his observation of genres is an observation of social behaviour. McAdams makes a stronger point than conformity to convention. His practical concern is the correlation between psychological wellbeing and particular narrative strategies. There is indeed a statistical association between certain narrative styles and mental health (e.g. McAdams *et al.*, 2001). It is reasonable to expect that someone prone to depression would 'keep going' a gloomy regressive narrative about self and world (on narrative and psychotherapy, see: McLeod, 1997; Crossley, 2000).

McAdams introduced his concept of the imago by distancing it from Jungian archetypes, noting that the archetypes catalogued in the Jungian literature include both personified and 'abstract or conceptual' ones (1985: 179). His examples: hero, wise old man, and earth mother, on the one side; birth, rebirth, death and power, on the other. His own concept is 'more specific' than archetype, for 'unlike Jung's structured components of the collective identity [*sic*], life-stories' imagoes are by definition personified and exist . . . as highly personalized, idiosyncratic images defining how a person is different from others as well as similar to them' (ibid.: 182–3). In McAdams' use, imagoes constitute a dimension of individual differences, like a personality trait. Someone might not realize that she describes herself as a warrior when telling about her life struggles, but this representation distinguishes her from someone who characterizes himself as a healer. However, Jung's concept is not 'more general' but radically different from McAdams' concept. As Hillman (1983: 66) observed, Jung is 'less concerned with personality as individualism than with individuation as an *impersonal* psychic process'. McAdams' 'imago' refers to a representation of oneself in one's story, whereas Jung uses the same word to indicate an intrapsychic state of subjective relation to world. In Jung's vocabulary, the archetype is a 'primordial image', where the word *image* (or *imago*) means 'not only the form of the activity taking place, but the typical situation in which the activity is released' (Jung, 1954, CW 9I: para. 152). Archetypal motifs found in life stories would not necessarily have the same significance from a Jungian viewpoint as from a narrative-psychological one.

In a conference paper, McAdams (2000) told of a middle-aged woman, Tanya, whose life story seemed premised on what he called a 'contamination' theme. Her happy childhood deteriorated to turbulent adolescence, substance abuse and more troubles. Tanya imposed this plot even on her high-point scene, the birth of her first child. Many people recall the birth of their first child as the high point of their life. But Tanya went on to mention how the child's father was found stabbed to death in a motel several years later. Although the son's birth and father's death were unconnected events separated in time, their juxtaposition in her narrative suggests a belief – a personal myth – that even when good things happen, bad things ruin them.

That myth could be contrasted with the belief that good comes out of bad, a 'redemption' theme, which McAdams illustrated with the life story of a middle-aged African American man, Jerome. From a 'Jungian' perspective, Tanya's story embodies an archetype of contamination and decay, whereas Jerome's story embodies an archetype of redemption and rebirth. Similar motifs are found throughout mythology, literature, drama and art – disengaged, as it were, from the life histories of their specific creators, reflecting universals of the human condition.

Narrative and the organization of experience

What is the scope for a post-Jungian narrative turn? The answer depends on how close to Jung's own thinking the would-be 'narrative Jungian' claims to be. Summing up the basic assumptions of narrative psychology, McAdams (1999) points out that most of its exponents, despite their differences, agree that selfhood is 'storied'. They concur that life stories organize disparate experience into integrated wholes, and that life stories are cultural texts. People tailor their life stories for particular audiences, and tell many stories, which change over time. Some stories are better than other stories in terms of mental health. Finally, the sharing of stories is viewed as building intimacy and community. It is not impossible to map analytical-psychological concerns onto that list, but the exercise would not capture the essence of Jung's thought. Jung's understanding of the literary is quite unlike the postmodernist literary metaphor of the self in narrative psychology. Whereas narrative psychology assumes an open-ended construction of personal identity (by means of narratives), Jung assumes the unfolding of a common-to-all psychic configuration (by means of images) – an unfolding that he regarded as a process of *individuation*. In Jungian use, the term 'individuation' means something different from the self-identity construction process that it implies in psychology generally and consequently in narrative psychology. Vincent Hevern defines narrative psychology as a viewpoint or stance premised on the notion that 'human activity and experience are filled with "meaning" and that stories, rather than logical arguments or lawful formulations, are the vehicle by which that meaning is communicated' (2006: online). Jung and narrative psychologists alike may hold that human activity and experience are filled with meaning, but whereas narrative psychologists regard 'stories, rather than logical arguments' as the vehicle for that meaning, Jung finds it in neither logical arguments nor personal stories.

One of the paradoxes of narrative psychology is that it does not investigate narrative as a phenomenon in its own right. Sarbin (1986) presented *narrative* as a new 'root' metaphor poised to replace the organic and mechanistic metaphors that had dominated psychology. He took the concept of the root metaphor from Pepper, who in 1942 described how worldviews develop. Desiring to understand the world, people may settle upon some commonsense fact and apply it to other areas, taking its structural characteristics as the basic conception of explanation and description: 'At first, metaphors are poetic creations. Once the metaphors are reified, frozen into tight belief patterns, metaphysical systems come into being' (ibid.: 5). Pepper identified six types of worldviews – animism, mysticism, formism, mechanism, organicism and contextualism – and considered the first two as irrelevant in modernity. The rest have their representatives also in psychology, as Sarbin points out. A 'formist' worldview stresses the organization of the world in terms of similarities and differences among things. The commonsense analogy is the craftsman who fashions similar products on the basis of the same plan, an implicit design or blueprint. Psychological exemplars include 'turn-of-the-century structuralism, contemporary personality trait theories, and the official doctrine of schizophrenia', according to Sarbin (ibid.: 6). In the mechanistic worldview, which is the metaphysical foundation of modern science, the root metaphor is the machine. Typical analogies include 'a clock, a dynamo, a computer, an internal combustion engine or a municipal water system' (ibid.: 6). Sarbin identifies behaviourism and radical empiricism as committed to that worldview. The scientific goal from the mechanistic viewpoint is to describe efficient causality. In contrast, when psychologists draw an analogy with the organism, their practices are premised on the assumption that an 'ideal structure is there to be discovered at the end of progressive steps or stages' and that the goal of the scientific inquiry is to 'locate parts within wholes' (ibid.: 6). Sarbin's examples include theories of self-actualization (Maslow), personal growth (Carl Rogers), and developmental theories based in notions of stages of maturation. Finally, Sarbin identifies contexualism as centred on the metaphor of the historical event. This is where he locates the narrative approach. To Sarbin, the historical event is not necessarily something that happened in the past, but a 'dynamic dramatic act' that is 'alive and in the present':

> The imagery called out by the historical event metaphor is that of an ongoing texture of multiply elaborated events, each leading to others, each being influenced by collateral episodes, and by the efforts of multiple agents who engage in actions to satisfy their needs and meet their obligations. Contained in the metaphor is the idea of constant change in the structure of situations and in positions occupied by actors.
>
> (Ibid.: 6)

However, as a loosely defined epistemology, contextualism was familiar in psychology long before postmodernism. Mostly American-led, with William James and John Dewey often cited as forerunners, it seeks to understand human behaviour in its natural setting. The designation 'contextualist' applies to frameworks that seek to describe the phenomenology of human action – but it equally applies to explaining rats' performance in lab experiments by contextualizing the behaviour in sequences of stimuli and consequences, as behaviourists do. To imagine 'narrative structures' as contexts for behaviour, as Sarbin does, we must make a postmodernist conversion to viewing human realities as constructed in language.

Sarbin contends that any event, insofar as it is lived meaningfully, is subordinate to narrative. We 'think, perceive, imagine, and make moral choices according to narrative structures'; and need only to 'reflect on any slice of life' in order to 'entertain seriously the proposal that the narratory principle guides thought and action' (ibid.: 8). At this juncture Sarbin refers to narrative in a literal sense. It is a means for 'organizing episodes, actions, and accounts of actions' that 'allows for the inclusion of actors' reasons for their acts, as well as the causes of happening' (ibid.: 9). As if compelled to elucidate by piling image upon image, Sarbin points out that

> In drama . . . we find a clear example of the historic act metaphor. The actors' performances, the setting, the time and place, the nature of audience, the script, the props, and so on, must all be taken into account to make sense of an episode or scene. . . . The meanings to be assigned to any actor's performance are a function of the context.
>
> (Ibid.: 7)

The analogy captures Sarbin's central claim: namely, that people see meaning in an action by seeing the action in the context of its happening, which in turns means having a 'story' about it. This re-indexes *narrative*, no longer as a metaphor or mere analogy for a psychological process, but as the process itself. The narrative metaphor thus collapses its source domain (whence it gets its imagery) and target domain (what it seeks to explain) into one. Analogies of a machine or organism, even a theatrical drama, draw upon our familiarity with something concrete that exists independently of the abstract concept that the metaphor is meant to communicate. Narrative is an abstract concept. It cannot be visualized, only grasped in another narrative.

The idea of narrative as a psychological process was articulated most extensively by Jerome Bruner. Contrasting 'narrative' and 'paradigmatic' (or logico-scientific) modes of thought, he suggested that both are fundamental and irreducible to each other. The paradigmatic is concerned with categorization, internal connections or logical relationships, and 'truth' in terms of a universal abstraction. The narrative mode is concerned with personal and social ramifications of events and relationships, strives to establish and affirm consensual meanings, and uses 'framing' devices so as to separate story from reality. It is involved in organizing and evaluating the vicissitudes of experience. Whereas the scientific explanation requires verification, 'in the domain of narrative and explication of human action we ask instead that, upon reflection, the account . . . "feel" as right' (Bruner, 1986: 52). Bruner (1990) identifies several features that distinguish a story from other forms of speech. It is 'basic' literary theory, but ultimately Bruner is after something else. His chapter-long account is interwoven with the implications for folk psychology (in social psychology: a field of study focused on people's ordinary explanations). The kind of stories whose features he is keen to specify is ordinary explanations of real events. The contrast with the Jungian focus on the imaginary hardly needs stating. According to Bruner, the principal characteristics of narrative are 'its sequentiality, its factual "indifference," and its unique way of managing departures from the canonical' (ibid.: 50). Discrete events and mental states are given a meaning by virtue of their placement in the whole, the plot or *fabula*, which in turn is extracted from the sequence. 'It is this unique sequentiality that is indispensable to a story's significance and to the mode of mental organization in terms of which it is grasped' (ibid.: 44). Since a story derives its effectiveness from the plot, it can be real or imaginary without losing its power as a story – a characteristic to which Bruner refers as an indifference to extralinguistic reality. Bruner further points out that narrative 'specializes in the forging of links between the exceptional and the ordinary' (ibid.: 47). It is when we are confronted with the unexpected or extraordinary that we tend to bring up some story that makes some sense of the situation: '*The function of the story is to find an intentional state that mitigates or at least makes comprehensible a deviation from a canonical cultural pattern*' (ibid.: 49–50; original emphasis). Further features of the well-formed narrative include what he calls its 'dual landscape'; that is, 'events and actions in a putative "real world" occur concurrently with mental events in the consciousness of the protagonists' (ibid.: 51). Bruner elaborates the dual-landscape point with an idea of 'subjunctivizing trans- formations', speculating that '"subjunctive" stories are easier to enter into, easier to identify with' (ibid.: 54). Noting that a story is *somebody's* story, Bruner surmises that stories are 'viable instruments for social negotiation' (ibid.: 54–5). Emily's social negotiation by means of her 'small stories' could be recalled here (see Chapter 2). Finally, noting that stories rely on tropes – such as metaphors, metonymies and other linguistic devices – Bruner points out that a story must be concrete. 'We interpret stories by verisimilitude, their "truth likeness", or more accurately, their "lifelike- ness"' (ibid.: 61).

Bruner acknowledges the role that storytelling convention and tradition may play in narrative structures. Yet he muses as to whether there is 'some human "readiness" for narrative that is responsible for conserving and elaborating such a tradition in the first place' – quickly inserting a disclaimer: 'By this I do not intend that we "store" specific archetypal stories or myths, as C. G. Jung has proposed' (ibid.: 45). And Jung had complained, 'My critics have incorrectly assumed that I am dealing with "inherited representations"' (1964: 57). Jung was hardly suggesting that we store stories or myths. He is more correctly understood as dealing with the readiness to *form* symbolic representation (sometimes by means of stories and myths) of typical human situations. Bruner's point is different. He conjectures a predisposition to organize actual experiences into narrative forms by way of explaining events. Our stories, inasmuch as they are *stories*, have certain characteristics regardless of the motifs that they might contain. Jung understands archetypal manifestations as *expressions* of subjective states; Bruner understands stories as *explanations*.

In support of Bruner's narrative/paradigmatic distinction, Polkinghorne (1989: 21) describes 'plot' as the means whereby people ordinarily explain actions:

> In narrative organization, the symmetry between explanation and prediction, characteristic of logico-mathematical reasoning, is broken. Narrative explanation does not subsume events under laws. Instead, it explains by clarifying the significance of events that have occurred on the basis of the outcome that has followed.

However, while a sequential ordering of events is an obvious criterion for distinguishing narratives from other forms of speech, that feature might not be the most important factor regarding the effectiveness of a narrative as an explanation. The idea that narrative is a form of speech that has a 'beginning, middle, and end' could be traced to Aristotle's recommendation for how the perfect tragedy ought to be structured. As a thing of beauty, the 'proper structure of the Plot . . . is that which has a beginning, a middle, and an end' (Aristotle, 1997[1895]: 14). To him, it was an ideal to aspire to; he chastised poets who wrote disjointed episodes. Discussing Aristotle's concept of a plot – or *mythos*, in Greek – Ricoeur (1984: 38) defines it as the 'logical character' of a story when taken as a whole. The tragic turn from good fortune to bad necessarily unfolds in story-time, but the *mythos* is the universal turn-of-fortune, not the particular sequence of events. By implication, the clarification of the significance of events on the basis of their outcome is but one practical use of narrative accounts. Forster (1974[1927]) distinguished between 'plot' and 'story': a story is a narrative of events, arranged in their time-sequence; it answers what happens next. A plot tells us *why*. His famous example: 'The king died, then the queen died' is a story; 'The king died, and then the queen died of grief' is a plot (ibid.: 60). Such narrative explains – not merely by presenting the queen's death as something that comes after the king's death – but through the sad *image* of the grieving queen, an image that takes us in. Walter Benjamin (1999[1936]) submitted that the power of a story lies in the extent to which it leaves us preoccupied with the protagonists' motives and feelings.

When considering whether Jung could be classed as a narrative psychologist, we should be mindful of how the same historical trends that gave rise to narrative psychology impacted also on Jungian studies. On the cusp of the formative decade for the narrative movement, Hillman (1983) cited Forster's story/plot distinction and pointed to the translation of *mythos* in Aristotle's writings as 'plot'. He concluded: 'Plots are myths. The basic answers to *why* are to be discovered in myths' (ibid.: 11). Hillman urges us to see the inner necessity of historical events in the events themselves – like Sarbin, as seen. As if echoing the sentiments that precipitated social constructionism, Hillman stresses that *inner* does not mean 'private and owned by a self' or a 'literalized place inside a subject', but instead means the 'subjectivity in events' and the attitude that 'interiorizes those events' (ibid.: 25). He adds, the 'core mistake of mechanism in [depth] psychology is that it literalizes functions and actions as discrete moving parts, separated from each other' (ibid.: 25) – again, as if participating (though he doesn't) in the paradigm shift from psyche to discourse. Ultimately his conclusion is different:

> But a mythos is more than a theory and more than a plot. It is the tale of the interaction of humans and the divine. To be in a mythos is to be inescapably linked with divine powers, and moreover, to be in mimesis with them.
>
> (Ibid.: 11)

What Hillman was actually saying might be intelligible only within his peculiar discourse of 'soul' and jargon contrived from Greek mythology, constituting his archetypal psychology, which is already removed from what Jung was saying.

We may come back to Jung via Greek philosophy, rather than mythology. To Aristotle, poetry expresses the universal; it tells of what could be; and is therefore a 'more philosophical and a higher thing than history', which informs about particular events that have happened (1997[1895]: 17). Similarly to Jung, myth or fantasy expresses psychological universals, and is therefore a 'higher thing' than autobiography. Fantasy is not exactly ignored by narrative psychologists – on the contrary, they often stress the importance of the imagination – but fiction is curiously evaded. It seems to be something of an embarrassment. Sarbin (1986: 11) suspected that because 'storytelling is commonly associated with fiction, fantasy, and pretending, some critics are skeptical about the use of the narrative as a model for thought and action'. Narrative researchers often claim to be less interested in the historical truth of their informants' stories than in how the story communicates meanings; but they nevertheless seek to describe real life as experienced by someone, not a life invented. Freeman (1997: 175) defended the study of autobiography in psychology with the contention that 'contra those who suppose that narrative entails a kind of fictive imposition on experience . . . it is more appropriately seen as being woven into the fabric of life itself'. It could be argued that writing modern fiction – unashamedly a fictive imposition on experience – serves to organize and find coherence in personal experience differently from how writing one's autobiography might (Jones, 2002b).

'The art teacher' and the form–function problem

Some of the themes discussed above and in the previous chapter may be pulled together with the aid of a case study, which in the first instance links to a point that Jung made, apropos of the Abbé Oegger story, regarding the conscious organization of unconscious material by means of conscious fantasies. Eight-year-old 'Adam' wrote the following story at the request of Nicola Critchlow (2003). She collected children's stories about classroom relationships as part of a Master's dissertation. The story is used here with permission and without reproducing Critchlow's analysis, which centred on the utility of the method. I corrected spelling errors and inserted some punctuation for ease of reading, and changed all the boys' names because the writer put himself and real classmates in the story (hence the repetition of Adam). There was no Mr Smife (possibly Smythe) in the school. Critchlow gave Adam a list of keywords: classroom; teacher; children; an incident; teacher's reactions; children's reactions. (Some children were given story stems instead.) The title is his creation.

The Art Teacher

One day Ben, Adam, Adam and Carl were going to school when they heard a car crash. So Ben, Adam, Adam and Carl found out it was the Art teacher Mr Smife.

'Mr Smife, are you OK?' said Ben. 'Yes, thank you for pulling me out,' said Mr Smife. 'By the way, Art lesson's first today.' 'Thanks Mr Smife,' said Adam and Adam.

After Assembly, Carl said, 'Art lesson's my favourite.' 'Mine too,' said Ben, Adam and Adam.

The next morning Mr Smife's car blew up and Mr Smife died. Ben, Adam, Adam and Carl were so sad, came to Mr Smife's funeral, and never did art again because the perfect art teacher was so good no art teacher was better.

Most of Adam's classmates wrote about realistic situations and moral issues. A story by another boy centred on a conflict between a teacher and a couple of boys who wanted to decorate the classroom with pictures of the footballer David Beckham. Another story, by a girl, told of a teacher refusing to deal with a boy who stole from a classmate until after the girls who reported it finished their work. When one of the girls chastised the boy herself, she was punished for bullying. Adam's story was not the only fantasy. Another boy wrote a sci-fi horror about giant mutant ants attacking the school. The boys organized themselves and heroically killed the ants, whilst the teachers were pathetically helpless (the female class teacher screamed and ran away at the beginning, and the headmaster was killed by an ant sitting on his head). Adam's story was unique in that the relationship between the teacher and the boys is very positive and symmetrical: the boys save him and he teaches them something they love. Why 'kill' him?

Applying Jungian principles to analyse nineteenth-century English novels, Dawson (2004) suggests that in each novel there is a figure, not necessarily the obvious hero, who pulls together all the elements of the novel into a coherent whole. That is the novel's *effective protagonist*. Dawson singles out the idea of 'compensation' as Jung's most important concept. Jung defined compensation as 'the unconscious of conscious activity' (1921, CW 6: para. 694) – that which we turn away from when turning towards something, so to speak. Jung stresses that compensation is not an escapist fantasy, but 'an actual fact that becomes still more actual the more we repress it' (1934, CW 16: para. 331). His concept rests on a view of the psyche as a relatively close 'self-regulating system that maintains its equilibrium just as the body does' (ibid.: para. 330) and which is composed of pairs of opposites. Understanding the psyche as a hermeneutic whole means that we don't need to go outside it in order to describe its dynamics. We need to identify its parts and their interrelations. In a similar vein, Dawson seeks to identify the way in which characters in a novel function in relation to each other. In Dawson's analyses, the protagonists complement each other as if horizontally or synchronically: they inhabit the plane of the story as a whole, including layers of subtext that give the story its depth. No additional information from outside the text has to be taken into account in order to understand how its elements are interrelated.

'The Art Teacher' could be considered along similar lines. It is ostensibly about Mr Smife, but he is not its hero. Adam put himself in his story, and it is tempting to consider him as the effective protagonist. But Adam-the-character is indistinguishable from the other boys. There is no obvious hero in this story, and no idealized self-image. Like a dream, it seems a snapshot of a subjective situation told in metaphor. 'The Art Teacher' has the simplicity of a fairytale. Compared with modern fiction, fairytale characters are two-dimensional, lacking psychological depth or 'voice'. Mr Smife and the boys have perfectly symmetrical functions: he is the victim, they are the rescuers; he is the perfect teacher, they are the keen pupils. In this way, teacher and boys *compensate* for something that the other lacks or cannot do. The story, its plot or mythos, derives its dynamic from the playing-out of their compensatory functions, leading to the dramatic disruption of the equilibrium. In one interpretation, its effective element is art itself. Art defines the relationship between the boys and the teacher. It also defines Ben, Adam, Adam and Carl as a single unit, unified in their attitude towards art lessons and the teacher. Yet, art does not inhabit the space of the story on equal terms with its five characters. It is not personified and is not even an event, for we don't follow the boys into the art lesson. It is visible to us only through the intensity and direction of affect expressed in their talk.

A different stance is called for when asking – as Jung did regarding dreams – what conscious attitude a story might unconsciously compensate for. In addressing this question, the story is approached as if diachronically or vertically: we may infer its function by looking 'under' it to examine the conditions for its creation and 'above' it to consider the consequences of its utterance. When Jung advised analysts to figure out what conscious attitude a dream might compensate for, he assumed that the dreamer is known to the analyst. The nexus on which compensatory elements are organized is *not* the story-space of the dream, but psychological continuities of its dreamer. Jung cautioned against jumping to conclusions based on a single dream of an unknown person. The directive is violated here when speculating about the significance of a single story by someone I never met, but the point of the present exercise is – not to 'analyse' that boy – but to examine what a text such as his imaginative story could be assumed to disclose. Jung suggested that conscious fantasies illustrate inner conflicts that are not recognized by the person at the time. There is a sense of foreclosure in Adam's story, a grieving for art. We don't know whether that was a crisis for the real boy. Critchlow spent time in the school before collecting the stories, getting to know the children, and recalled that he liked art. But her fieldwork was done before I read the material, and we couldn't find out more about him. We are left with a textual abstraction, a schoolboy imagined by us through this single story. Only the general circumstances of the production of the story are known. It was written in the classroom. The children were used to writing creative stories, and the teacher encouraged them to write 'interesting' ones (I'm told). Adam is a sophisticated storyteller with a dramatic flair. As if adhering to Aristotle's description of the perfect tragedy in *Poetics*, his story makes its impact through a surprising reversal of fortune. The repetition of 'Ben, Adam, Adam and Carl' has the ring of oral storytelling. It is highly plausible that he had an actual audience in those classmates. The researcher noticed that children showed their stories to each other. Quite a few put their friends in the story, some making deliberate in-jokes about each other. A motivation to write an 'interesting' story coupled with writing for a known audience make this story unlike a dream, and prompt our attention to the dialogic dimension (as defined in the previous chapter).

Although under the circumstances it is impossible to know the real significance of 'The Art Teacher' for its writer, the utterance of the story inevitably positions him in specific ways within his social milieu. In having Adam-the-character as 'one of the lads', the story performs social affiliation. The act is performed not by telling *about* friendship or camaraderie, but by virtue of what the story takes for granted: that Adam and his friends do everything together and feel the same. If consciously Adam is one of the lads, could 'The Art Teacher' be compensating for an unconscious sense of isolation in his love of art? This possibility invites a classification of the story as a tragedy for other reasons than its sad ending. Northrop Frye placed the hero's isolation at the heart of tragedy. Tragic heroes are 'wrapped in the mystery of their communion' with something that we see only through their struggle, and that something is the 'source of their strength and fate alike' (Frye, 1957: 208). Perhaps Adam's struggle is with a feeling that art is incompatible with masculine identity. To Frye, comedy as a literary genre is about attempts at social integration. Such attempt is implicit, not in the literal text of 'The Art Teacher', but in its dialogic dimension. In a way, the story informs Ben, Carl, and the other Adam that he is growing out of childish things like art just like them. They share the adventure and irreversible loss of growing up.

Fantasies can be analysed either with a focus on their text or with a view to learning about the fantasizing person. These are alternative analytic strategies, not rival theories about the meaning of a particular text. The analytic tool that Dawson derived from Jung's theory can be used by other literary critics who (unlike Dawson) are inclined to dismiss the Jungian model of the psyche. Pinpointing the effective protagonist in a novel doesn't commit the scholar to speculating about the novelist's mind. In contrast, when we ask about the fantasizing person, we need external information. Speculations about the dialogic function of the utterance of Adam's story cannot be made on the basis of its text alone (I had to know something about the circumstances of its production). When conceptual tools derived from Jung are used in a psychological inquiry, we must either accept his model of the psyche or, if we reject it, propose an alternative that explains why we believe that these tools are viable despite Jung's being wrong. The irony is that when we are taken by a different 'picture' of the self we might not see the need for tools such as his in the first place. 'The Art Teacher' would be of little interest in narrative psychology, for instance. To paraphrase one of Jung's observations apropos of Abbé Oegger: from the narrative standpoint we are less inclined to ask how (fictional) texts express the universal and ever-renewed thoughts of mankind than to ask how (autobiographical) texts perpetuate accounts of ordinary everyday events in the personal past.

Another lesson of 'The Art Teacher' is that when we focus on the singular text, its author as imagined by us is a narrative construction, a character in a story that we tell. It is 'the universalizing of the plot that universalizes the characters, even when they have specific names' (Ricoeur, 1984: 41). When universal mechanisms of the fantasizing mind are inferred from the universalized plot of someone's fiction or dream, we might lose sight of the involvement of a living consciousness – our own – that apprehends a recurrence, regularity and pattern in a series of texts.

From his standpoint as a literary critic, Frye regarded archetypes as highly communicative narrative images in novels: the archetype is 'a symbol, usually an image, which recurs often enough in literature to be recognizable as an element of one's literary experience as a whole' (1957: 365). In support of Frye, Ricoeur (1984: 18) comments that we 'should not rush to denounce the latent "Jungianism" of the archetypal criticism'. In Frye's use, the term archetype emphasizes 'the recurrence of the same verbal forms' and this recurrence 'contributes to the unification and integration of our literary experience' (ibid.: 18). Jung, in his approach to the literary, was less concerned with the literary experience than with explaining why certain literary forms exist; that is, what is their psychological function.

If Frye or Ricoeur define an archetype as a recurrent narrative unit that recurs because it is communicatively effective, Jung's theory purports to explain *why* it is so effective. Perhaps it is effective because it delivers a subjective situation to consciousness in a capsule form. However, when recurrent elements are identified solely in terms of textual forms, it is difficult to 'get back' to their subjective functions. There is no permanent correspondence between certain motifs in literary works and the function of the particular motif for the writer. For example, drawing upon Freud, Jung and Lévi-Strauss, Abarbanell (1994) identified dualistic images of the woman in fiction by Amalia Kahana-Carmon, an Israeli woman writer, and some other Israeli (male) writers. These motifs could be found in Kahana-Carmon's fiction, but the discovery tells us nothing about what her fiction is actually about. Most scholars who study her fiction tend to highlight its 'woman's voice', which sets it apart from fiction by male writers. Separately, Annis Pratt (1981) examined women's fiction spanning several centuries. She draws upon Jung's theory, but instead of mining the literary works for the archetypes specified by Jung, Pratt derives archetypes that are suggested by the material at hand. She delineates several recurrent themes that correspond to typical experiences of women in patriarchal societies. For instance, a 'green-world archetype' (citing Simone de Beauvoire): the adolescent girl '"will devote a special love to Nature. . . . Unconquered, inhuman Nature subsumes most clearly the totality of what exists" . . . Later, the mature woman hero tends to look back to moments of natural-istic epiphany as touchstones in a quest for her lost selfhood' (ibid.: 16–17). Kahana-Carmon writes about stations of womanhood such as identified by Pratt, but there is no earthy green-world (and its pagan undertones) in her fiction. Instead, her heroines find moments of naturalistic epiphany in 'the heavenly splendour of the sky, with its dawns, sunsets and, above all, light, which has undertones of Jewish mysticism' (Jones, 2002b: 97). If we inquire about the significance of the theme for Kahana-Carmon herself, we would enter the domain of psychological (or more broadly social-scientific) inquiries, and would need to know something about her as a person.

Closing comments

The failure of agreement between Jung and Bakhtin, pointed out at the beginning of the chapter, could be attributed to a mismatch between the traditional concerns of psychology and those of the *Geisteswissenschaften*. A literary work is approached in fundamentally different ways by psychologists as opposed to literary critics: 'What is of decisive importance and value for the latter may be quite irrelevant for the former,' says Jung (1950, CW 15: para. 136). Bakhtin is characteristically less dogmatic. He comments in notes made in his last years, 'Thoughts about thoughts, experiences of experiences, words about words. Herein lies the basic distinction between our disciplines (human sciences) and the natural ones (about nature), although there are no absolute, impenetrable boundaries here' (Bakhtin, 1981: 103). Those boundaries become even more permeable in narrative psychology, though its own gravity centre has shifted away from literature as such. We may agree with Bakhtin that it is misguided to locate the truth of human situations in the 'repeatable and constant' and to assume that the 'universal and identical . . . is fundamental and essential' – especially when the array of instances under comparison are *representations* of human situations (e.g. literary). But the issue is not clear-cut. How do such images come into being in the first place? Why? What's their function?

Those are psychological questions, with which Jung was deeply engaged, and which seem neglected in postmodern psychology. His answer – the theory of archetypes – is problematic. It is ambiguous partly because it underwent changes in Jung's own writings. He refined the theory over several decades, and what he ended up saying (or could be heard as saying) became channelled by the specific terminology that he hit upon at some point around 1920. The word 'archetype' has different connotations from those of the clumsier phrase 'primordial image', which Jung continued to use as interchangeable but which was generally abandoned by his followers. 'Archetype' loses the explicit reference to *image*, with its connotations of representation, seeing, hence of a beholder and subjectivity. Instead, it alludes to a structure that exists in itself, independently of any observation. In philosophy, the term archetype is closely associated with Platonic Ideas. Jung both anchored his concept in Plato and laboured to dissociate it from Plato (cf. Jones, 2003b). Unlike Plato, his hypothesis rests on an assumption of isomorphic physiological evolution and the evolution of the psyche or mind. In biology, the term was used to represent 'selected clusters of conserved features' based on body plan characteristics (Richardson, Minelli and Coates, quoted in Jones, 2003d: 707). The biologists list examples such as 'Owen's vertebrate archetype, Urbilateria (the archetypal ancestor of triploblastic bilateral metazoans) and single structures such as the penta-dactylous tetrapod limb' (ibid.: 707). Jung may have known of Owen's archetypes, though he doesn't mention it (as far as I know). The termin-ology reinforces his physiological analogy of the psyche (citations in the next chapter). He assumed that, just as anatomies evolve when sophis-ticated structures are added onto primitive ones, so there must be living fossil structures within the psyche. Just as primitive anatomical structures remain functionally integrated in the workings of the present-day living organism, so intrapsychic archetypal structures remain functional, con-stituting 'the inherited possibility of psychic functioning in general' (Jung, 1921, CW 6: para. 842). Unlike Owen's archetypes and similar examples from physiology, however, Jungian archetypes are characterized by considerable flexibility of form–function relations. The same mythological motif could serve different psychological functions under different circum-stances; and, conversely, a similar function could be served by different imagery.

Archetype theory thus confronts a dilemma in terms of its utility for psychological inquiries. On the one hand, it alludes to the possibility of a universal index for typical human situations that become expressed in particular motifs that are indicative of corresponding psychological func-tions with respect to those situations. On the other, its applicability to individual cases requires our readiness to abandon that very notion. Jung himself warns about taking form–function bonds too rigidly; e.g. against connecting 'a dream about a snake with the mythological occurrence of snakes, for who is to guarantee that the functional meaning of the snake in the dream is the same as in the mythological setting?' (1954, CW 9I: para. 103). If the practical aim was to create a diagnostic manual of sorts, Jung failed. But it is debatable whether that was ever his intention. The 'fluid' or indeterminable association between any specific form and specific function is a crucial theoretical point concerning the nature of human under-standing.

Chapter 4

Two models: the dialogical self and dynamical psyche

That would be the picture of our psychic structure.

(Jung, 1931, CW 10: para. 54)

What this language primarily describes is a picture. What is to be done with the picture, how it is to be used . . . must be explored if we want to understand the sense of what we are saying. But the picture seems to spare us this work: it already points to a particular use. This is how it takes us in.

(Wittgenstein, 1953: 184)

The Dutch psychotherapist Hubert Hermans and associates presented the 'dialogical self' model in a book (Hermans and Kempen, 1993) and numerous journal-papers (e.g. Hermans, 1999, 2001a, 2001b; Hermans *et al.*, 1992). To date, Hermans seems to be the only major postmodern psychologist to make contact with the Jungian world. When he began to disseminate his theory, he published also in the *Journal of Analytical Psychology* (Hermans, 1993). A decade later, the Jungian analyst John Beebe (2002) contributed to a Special Issue of *Theory and Psychology* that Hermans edited as a guest editor. Contact does not always mean a dialogue, however. Hermans' paper and Beebe's review provide a narrative bridge (not a synthesis) between Jungian and postmodern perspectives, but it is a bridge that should make us aware of the chasm between them.

Beebe (2002) interprets Hermans' model as akin to Jung's theory of the complexes and their archetypal bases. He sums up Hermans' theory as the idea of feeling-toned standpoints that dominate a person's consciousness 'in the parade of complex-driven states of mind'; Hermans envisages a 'Heraclitean flux . . . produced by the way the complexes of the psyche continually replace each other in an endless round' (ibid.: 269). Although that is accurate enough, Hermans himself does not use the word *complexes*. Beebe's review leads to introducing his own model of the psyche as comprising paired archetypal opposites (see also Beebe, 2006). It stands on its Jungian feet, taking nothing from Hermans, and indeed resisting the assumptions that define Hermans' approach as 'dialogical'. Hermans takes nothing from Jung in developing his own model. The separate intellectual paths that he and Jung follow draw near in a conception of 'moving opposites in the self' (from the title of Hermans' 1993 paper). Addressing Jungian analysts, Hermans optimistically suggested that his approach 'ought to clarify Jung's position on the phenomenon of opposites and the ultimate style of their "reconciliation"' (ibid.: 460). The Jungian world in general was unresponsive, perhaps because Hermans did not make it clear what needed clarifying about Jung's position. In that paper, he acknowledges Jung's idea of paired opposites alongside others' ideas of personality dualities (elsewhere Jung is dropped from the list), but the report of Jungian theory is based on McAdams' (1985) review. As indicated in the previous chapter, McAdams' review is not quite in tune with Jung. Moreover, because McAdams sought to differentiate his 'imago' concept from Jungian archetypes, his review omits some aspects of Jung's theory that would be the most relevant with regard to Hermans' theory.

Turning to McAdams for information about Jung reveals Hermans' primary affiliation: the narrative movement of the 1980s. In their book, Hermans and Kempen (1993) firmly base the 'dialogical self' in the central resources and canonical texts of narrative psychology. They also draw on G. H. Mead (though with reservations) and on Vico. They mostly reiterate discussions by other postmodern scholars. The originality and creativity of Hermans' model lie in the assimilation of the intellectual resources of postmodern psychology towards an application in psychotherapy. The model is associated with a structured technique, the Self-Confrontation Method. When addressing non-Jungian audiences, Hermans seldom makes the Heraclitean reference (it doesn't 'resonate' in this context), but he is consistent in his view of personal meaning as emergent from a movement between opposite subject positions. The picture that takes us in when Hermans' model resonates with postmodern sensitivities is the vivid depiction of multivoicedness:

> The dialogical self, in contrast with the individualistic self, is based on the assumption that there are many *I* positions that can be subsumed by the same person. The *I* in one position can agree, disagree, understand, misunderstand, oppose, contradict, question, and even ridicule the *I* in another position.
>
> (Hermans *et al.*, 1992: 29)

As early as 1916, Jung suggested that the relationship between the conscious and the unconscious is 'exactly as if a dialogue were taking place between two human beings' and went on to say,

The shuttling to and fro of arguments and affects represents the transcendent function of opposites. The confrontation of the two positions generates a tension charged with energy and creates a living thing, a third . . . that leads to a new level of being, a new situation.

(Jung, 1958, CW 8: para. 189)

But the convergence of analogies must not detract from their divergent statements concerning the nature of human nature.

In psychology, 'one of the most important phenomena is the *statement* . . . our subtlest lucubrations can establish no more than is expressed in the statement: this is how the psyche behaves,' commented Jung (1948, CW 9I: para. 384). What is a statement, exactly? Deleuze (1988: 18) suggests that 'statements resemble dreams and are transformed in a kaleidoscope, depending on the corpus in question and the diagonal line being followed' between strata of knowledge formation. He refers to Foucault's concept. In *The Archaeology of Knowledge*, Foucault (1989[1969]) defines it through a series of negatives: statements are not propositions, sentences or speech acts. Foucault insists that the statement is not a linguistic unit. It would be misguided to speak of an 'atomic' statement 'with its apparent meaning, its origins, its limits, and its individuality' (ibid.: 120). The two models reviewed below each consist of definite propositions, defining its origins, boundaries and individuality – but are perhaps best viewed as statements in the elusive Foucauldian sense. 'The statement is neither visible nor hidden,' continues Foucault (ibid.: 122). It is not visible, for it is not given as a grammatical or logical structure of what is said or written. It is not hidden, for there is no secret meaning behind it. Even blanks or gaps that it contains indicate its 'presence in the space of dispersion that constitutes the "family"' of statements, explains Deleuze (1988: 16). Deleuze suggests that a family of statements is formed by 'rules of change or variation' that make it 'a medium for dispersion and heterogeneity, the very opposite of homogeneity' (ibid.: 5). Jung's approach belongs in a family of statements that are dispersed within a space of questions different from that in which Hermans' approach belongs. Consequently, similar claims might have dissimilar meanings for their authors. When Jung says that the psyche is characterized by disunity, his claim challenges or supports different assumptions from those challenged or supported by Hermans when he makes a similar claim about the self. Foucault urges us to seek the rules of discursive formations in discourse itself, but he doesn't reduce everything to discourse. His example, clinical medicine at the end of the eighteenth century, is a discursive formation, but it is related to the formation of non-discursive environments, such as institutions and their physical structures, as well as political events and economic practices. Deleuze draws the distinction more sharply. On the one side are statements, which are not directed towards anything and do not relate to something as its outward expression; they exist solely within language. On the other side Deleuze places non-discursive 'forms, proportions and perspectives that are . . . free of any intentional gaze', which he calls 'visibilities' (1988: 109).

Deleuze concludes, 'All knowledge runs from a visible element to an articulable one, and vice versa' (ibid.: 39). The formation of the knowledge that Jung and Hermans separately provide runs between the visible and the articulable, not only in terms of an interplay between these authors' theorizing and clinical observations, but also in their deployment of heuristic imagery in the effort to articulate what seems to them visible in the empirical facts. Models of the self or psyche, however rationally they are reasoned out, involve 'picturing' what is being spoken about – and the picture takes us in, as Wittgenstein pointed out.

Parts of psyche

Beebe (2002) begins his review of Hermans' theory by citing sources tracing the Western idea of multiple centres of awareness to Homer in Ancient Greece and to Nietzsche. He notes that Jung, when developing the theory of the complexes, also drew upon views of mental dissociation expounded by Flournoy, Pierre Janet and William James, among others. This 'rich intellectual tradition' provides the background for Hermans' explication of the dynamics of the dialogical self, observes Beebe (ibid.: 269). Hermans himself does not contextualize his theory in relation to that European tradition (and takes something different from William James, as will be seen). The dialogical self is introduced in Hermans and Kempen (1993) and elsewhere as a new idea based in a worldview that is discontinuous with previous worldviews in psychology and psychotherapy. Based on a critique by Sampson (1985), Hermans and Kempen contend that the self was assumed to be unitary and centralized until the late twentieth century. Jung surely cannot be accused of such assumption. Jung held that the psyche is 'not an indivisible unity but . . . a divided whole', whose separate parts, although they are interconnected, are 'relatively independent, so much so that certain parts of psyche never become associated with the ego at all, or very rarely' (1948a, CW 8: para. 582). He too identified a shift away from notions of a centralized self – but it was a century earlier: 'it is only since the end of the nineteenth century that modern psychology . . . proved empirically the existence of a psyche outside consciousness. With this discovery the position of the ego . . . became relativized' (1951, CW 9II: para. 11).

What precisely are the parts of the psyche according to Jung depends on whether we consult his earlier or later writings. Initially he described autonomous *complexes*, defined as clusters of emotionally toned ideas:

> Everyone knows nowadays that people 'have complexes.' What is not so well known, though far more important theoretically, is that

complexes can *have us*. The existence of complexes throws serious doubts on the naïve assumption of the unity of consciousness, which is equated with 'psyche', and on the supremacy of the will.

(Jung, 1934, CW 8: para. 200)

Following Pierre Janet and others, Jung describes those as 'splinter psyches' that have a consciousness of their own – cautioning that this 'metaphorical paraphrase of a scientific problem' should be taken 'with a very large grain of salt' (ibid.: para. 203). Defined more fully,

> [A] 'feeling-toned complex' is . . . the *image* of a certain psychic situation which is strongly accentuated emotionally and is, moreover, incompatible with the habitual attitude of the consciousness. This image has a powerful inner coherence, it has its own wholeness and, in addition, a relatively high degree of autonomy . . . The complex can usually be suppressed with an effort of will, but not argued out of existence.

(Ibid.: para. 201)

Jung claimed to have discovered the complexes by means of word association tests. The basic technique is widely used in cognitive psychology with attention to common patterns. For instance, the fact that most people would associate the word 'bread' with 'butter' more quickly than with other words, or react more slowly to emotionally loaded words such as 'war' or 'rape' than to neutral words. Jung was more interested in individual-specific response patterns, on grounds that hesitation on particular words indicates unconscious barriers. Following Janet, he attributed the formation of the 'splinter psyches' to fragmentation due to a trauma.

Jung was already known for his work on the complexes before teaming up with Freud and before hitting upon the idea of the collective unconscious. Subsequent to postulating the collective unconscious, the notion of complexes acquired an additional dimension of meaning for Jung, which progressively took over his attention and eventually seemed to suppress talk of complexes altogether. His later theory superimposes upon the horizontal array of personal complexes a vertical axis, polarized in terms of personal versus collective unconscious. Now the complexes can be envisaged as forming around archetypal nuclei or 'primordial images'. Whereas the early Jung seemed interested in the particular contents of individuals' complexes, the later Jung became far more interested in a universal (and therefore impersonal) blueprint for all personalities. His voluminous writings on archetypes are devoted to identifying those common-to-all parts of the psyche. His definition of archetypes as *'forms without content . . . the possibility of a certain type of perception and action'* (1954, CW 9I: para. 99) means that they can't be 'complexes', if complexes are to be understood as clusters of emotionally toned ideations (i.e. definite contents). The inter-relation of these concepts could be illustrated as follows. All humans are born instinctually disposed to form an attachment to a caregiver, a pre-disposition that has specific physiological, behavioural and cognitive expressions. It could be assumed therefore that there is a readiness to *experience* oneself in 'attachment' situations. That would be the archetype-as-such, the form without content. The dualities of being loved/rejected, nourished/neglected and secure/insecure find expressions in diverse cultural representations of the 'loving and terrible mother' (ibid.: para. 158). That would be archetypal manifestations. The mother-complex would consist of personal contents that coalesce as a result of the real-life relationship with actual caregivers. Few of the other archetypes identified by Jung could be anchored in human biology so conveniently, however.

Referring to Jung's early work, Rapaport (1951: 221, n. 62) commented that the concept of complexes 'never reached full clarity and was soon abandoned by psychoanalysis'. The idea that thought processes involve the auto-organization of knowledge into differentiated structures – called mental schemas, scripts, inner working models and more – has remained central in mainstream psychology to the present day. Rapaport's grounds for dismissing 'complexes' warrant a closer look. As seen in Chapter 2, Silberer took from Jung the notion that normally the ego-complex inhibits other complexes during wakefulness:

> To suppress a complex means to deprive it of its attention-cathexis, its clarity. Therefore, the complexes must get along in their thinking with just a fraction of clarity. This allows only for vague and symbolic expressions, which consequently lack distinction and merge easily.
>
> (Jung [1907] as quoted in Silberer, 1951[1912]: 223)

Rapaport points out that cathexis (*Besetzung*) literally means 'charge'. In other words, Jung was describing what happens when most of the mind's energy is channelled into the ego, as in ordinary wakefulness. That parti-cular metaphor of energy lost its vitality by the time that Rapaport was writing. Rapaport contended,

> The notion that complexes can 'think' . . . would be untenable today. The thought-process is now conceived as integral and indivisible; but its manifest forms may show continuity (as in normal thought) or discontinuity (as in fugues), logical orderedness (as in normal thought) or symbolical orderedness (as in dreams, reveries, delusional states).
>
> (Ibid.: 223, n. 73)

The viewpoint gaining momentum at the time of Rapaport's writing became more clearly expressed in the computer metaphor a couple of decades later. Influenced by that metaphor, self-concept models developed during the 1970s and 1980s posit a mental structure for processing information about oneself. In the course of growing up, such structure becomes differentiated into specialized domains, such as beliefs about one's own academic competence, social relationships, physical attractiveness and more (for a Jung-relevant review, see Jones, 2004).

The cognitivist notion of self-concept domains is not the same idea as the complexes (or 'splinter' personalities) that Jung hypothesized and which Hermans brings back with a postmodernist twist – but all three can be linked to William James. Authors of self-concept models often acknowledge their debt to James' description of the 'empirical self' ('me') as comprising 'selves' that correspond to discrete aspects of experiencing oneself. James identified material, social and spiritual selves. The material self refers to one's body, clothes, house and so on. The social self is the recognition that one receives from others. James defined the spiritual self, not in religious terms (though it is related to religiosity) but as the result of 'our having become able to think of subjectivity as such, *to think ourselves as thinkers*' (1890: I, 296). James further spoke of 'rivalry' between the selves – an anthropomorphism echoed in Hermans' claim that the *I* in different positions 'can agree, disagree, understand, misunderstand, oppose, contradict, question, and even ridicule' each other (as seen). Hermans (e.g. 2001a) takes from James, not the idea of discrete domains, but the view of the self as 'extended' into the social environment. James (1890: I, 294) submitted that '*a man has as many social selves as there are individuals who recognize him* and carry an image of him in their mind' (original emphasis). In his turn to James, Hermans cites only the social and material selves. The inward-turned spiritual self is obviously not 'extended', though James considered it as fundamental for our self-experiencing as are the other domains. It is as if Hermans started off with a view of the self as entirely social-relational (cf. Mead) and took from James only that which confirms it. James' material domain clearly blurs into the social, for one's body and possessions are often associated with self-presentation, social status or stigma. Whereas Hermans' description of the self seems blind to the domain that James called the spiritual self, Jung's description of the self could be viewed as located solely in that domain (and is blind to the social). 'The self . . . is a God-image, or at least cannot be distinguished from one' (Jung, 1951, CW 9II: para. 42).

By the time that he made that bold claim, Jung too stopped speaking about complexes. In a major later work of his, *Aion* (1950, CW 9II), Jung limits the parts of the self to an ego, shadow (its unconscious opposite) and the syzygy (the anima/animus parts of male/female personalities). However, to Jung, the self (*Selbst*) is not the same as the psyche (or *Seele*). The self is an archetype, an abstract concept of a 'whole' being, which was intuited throughout cultures and epochs and is symbolically represented in various ways. *Aion* traces its transformations in the Christian aeon, although it is in Buddhism and Hinduism that Jung finds an iconography for the self; namely, the geometric patterns of a mandala. The self and its parts are only some of the archetypes described by Jung. It is not clear how the mother, child, trickster, wise old man, rebirth and other archetypes should be placed in relation to the self and its parts (but for a suggestion going beyond Jung, see Beebe, 2002, 2006). What seems clear is that such parts are not extended into the environment in the sense that Hermans or James speak of the extended self. Rather, these are *projected* externally. Jung regards the mechanism of projection as necessary for the integration of the self (individuation). 'The shadow can be realized only through a relation to a partner, and anima and animus only through a relation to a partner of the opposite sex' (Jung, 1951, CW 9II: para. 42). An unconscious element can be brought to consciousness only when seen in other people and is recognized as a projection (as opposed to believing it to be a trait of the other person). We need other people in order to see our own self – but we need them instrumentally, like needing a mirror with which to see our face. That's different from the viewpoint articulated by Mead and embraced also by Hermans, that we can become 'selves' only within contexts of experience shared with others – that, by analogy, we have no face without the mirror.

Voices of the self

Gergen (1997) identified Hermans' approach as a major variant of thought within social constructionism, alongside Harré's and his own. To paraphrase Wittgenstein, theirs is an agreement in form of life, not in opinions about the nature of the self. Whereas Harré sees a flow of discourse, and sees persons as locations for discursive events, Hermans sees real people in perpetual oscillations of personal dualities. If Harré's standpoint shatters the self into a panorama of fleeting Meadian 'me's glimpsed in conversation (as seen in Chapter 2), Hermans' standpoint puts it back together again by assuming that a coherent self-narrative can emerge from the continual flow of ever-shifting I-positions. Unlike either Harré or Gergen, Hermans' theorizing is subordinate to its application in psychotherapy, and is therefore driven by pragmatic concerns such as how to identify a client's array of I-positions and how to facilitate the therapeutic goal of self-integration.

Hermans and co-writers provide the best defence of their thesis in detailed clinical case studies. Suffice it to relate one example, which Hermans (2000) tells anecdotally. During therapy it was established that a certain client thought of himself alternatively as an avenger or as a dreamer. Asked to tell his life story from the position of the avenger, he recalled experiences with dishonest people, his impulsive and over-emotional father, and the disappointing behaviour of his girlfriend. Those experiences were associated with anger, powerlessness, disappointment and loneliness. As the dreamer, he described himself as a rescuer of the world, and told of idealized relationships, extraordinary achievements in his job and the most beautiful moments he had with his girlfriend. These experiences were associated with enjoyment, trust, energy, happiness and pride. Hermans tells the case in a commentary concerning methodological issues in narratology. The anecdote illustrates the contingency of any particular self-identity abstracted from a life story told in a research interview. Reading it through a Jungian lens, a more vivid illustration of Jung's claim that our complexes can 'have us' could hardly be imagined. However, the dreamer and avenger in this context are less like Jungian complexes (or arguably nothing like those) and more like McAdams' imagoes: i.e. idealized self-images in personal stories. Hermans goes beyond narrativism by implying that it is the emotions that have us, so to speak. 'The person is not simply a storyteller, but a passionate storyteller. . . . Typically, clients do not tell their stories as though they are exploring a free space, but focus on those parts that arouse affect or even strong emotions' (Hermans, 1999: 1193).

One of Hermans' core contentions is the importance of the imagination, which he makes repeatedly in various publications. When he refers to the imaginal, however, he means something different from what the word tends to imply in Jungian contexts. Hillman (1975: 37) assigns to depth psychology the task of differentiating 'the imaginal, discovering its laws, its configurations and moods of discourse, its psychological necessities'. That task has been typically empiricized in archetypal analyses that may show us the hero with a thousand faces (to borrow Joseph Campbell's phrase) – but it doesn't show us a real person who regards himself as a rescuer of the world, like Hermans' aforementioned client. Hermans indirectly (for he doesn't make it his point) counteracts the facelessness of the thousand-faced hero by giving voices to the many ways in which people imagine themselves into their actual life situations. Stressing the importance of 'imaginal dialogues', he means imagined conversations with real or imaginary people. 'Imaginal others' are found not only in the work of artists, but in anyone, and can be explored empirically. These would be one's family, friends and other real people (as one imagines them), imaginary characters, or ways of being that are 'not-me'. Such others occupy positions in relation to self in one's imagination: '*I* construe another person or being as a position that *I* can occupy and a position that creates an alternative perspective on the world and myself' (Hermans *et al.*, 1992: 29). Moreover, one's 'self' in one set of circumstances can function like the 'other' in another set of circumstances. Put together, such self–other multiplicities constitute an 'imaginal space'. It is intrinsically social. To paraphrase Hillman, the 'laws, configurations, moods of discourse, and psychological necessities' of the imaginal space that Hermans envisages are the characteristics of someone's social world as experienced by that person.

The Self-Confrontation Method that Hermans devised for clinical application pivots on a concept of *valuation*. Valuation is operationalized as a narrative unit that implies a pattern of affect. 'A valuation is any unit of meaning that has a positive (pleasant), negative (unpleasant) or ambivalent (both pleasant and unpleasant) value in the eyes of the individual' (Hermans and Kempen, 1993: 148). The theory delineates a 'manifest or surface' level of functioning, characterized by the 'phenomenological variety of narratives'; and a 'latent or deep' level, characterized by 'a limited number of basic forces or motives . . . influencing the content and organization of the stories on the manifest level' (ibid.: 148). Valuations that are manifest in personal accounts reflect the dynamics of two basic and contradictory motives, which he calls *striving for self-enhancement* (S motive) and *longing for contact and union* with others (O motive). As seen in the previous chapter, McAdams similarly found that life stories could be classified in terms of their emphasis on 'agency' versus 'communion'. Whereas for McAdams the distinction indicates differences between people (some people are agency oriented, others are communion oriented), Hermans points to oscillations between the two orientations within the individual. Hermans and Kempen infuse the above with the 'image' of multivoicedness:

> The central basic idea . . . is that *each I position has its own valuation system* and that valuations constructed from the perspective of a particular position can be considered as *utterances* that can be exchanged with the valuations of other positions. In this way different positions are able to influence the valuations of the other positions in a dialogical fashion.
>
> (Ibid.: 149; original emphasis)

When Hermans is read through a Jungian lens, the I-positions with their valuation systems might seem like Jung's complexes under another label.

In almost identical language as used by Jung to describe the complexes, Herman and Kempen posit 'unconscious positions [that] represent more or less autonomous centres of self-organization', and submit that

> [The] unconscious can become 'dialogicized,' that is, the suppressed or even split off positions can be taken up in the process of dialogue by giving them a voice, establishing a more symmetrical relation among conscious and unconscious positions. This can only happen when psychologists have available strategies and techniques that, together with their personal qualities, have enough dialogical power to stimulate the dominated positions to enter into the process of exchange.
>
> (Ibid.: 164)

The 'dialogicizing' process sounds very similar to the process that Jung regarded as happening naturally in dreams; and he too held that psychologists need strategies, techniques and personal qualities with which to guide their clients towards a more symmetrical relation between conscious and unconscious parts. Hermans and Kempen object to the 'misleading notion of a razor sharp boundary between conscious and unconscious', stating that they 'prefer to speak different levels of consciousness' (ibid.: 164). The sharp distinction is perhaps too readily made in Jungian studies – and is crystallized in the 'transcendent function' postulate – but Jung's differentiation between complexes in terms of relative clarity suggests a more nuanced view. One conspicuous difference between the two models is that there is no equivalent for the collective unconscious in Hermans' theorizing. He does not assume innate propensities to form certain kinds of I-positions.

Another difference is that Hermans resists the notion that inner harmony or equilibrium is a natural developmental goal. Unlike Jung, Hermans does not postulate 'a supraordinate, unified self as the driving force of individuation' (Beebe, 2002: 269). Jung's description of the structure of the psyche evolved over many decades, with later concepts enveloping earlier ones in his writings. He did not retract the trauma explanation of 'splinter psyches' when reviewing the theory of the complexes more than twenty years after coming up with the collective-unconscious hypothesis (see Jung, 1934, CW 8). Instead, the 'trauma' explanation merged with an assumption of a cultural 'pathogenic conflict' – a 'disunity with oneself is the hall-mark of civilized man', which he attributed to the 'progressive subjugation of the animal in man' due to the growth of culture (1943, CW 7: para. 17). Neurosis transpires as an unsuccessful attempt to resolve the disunity that we all suffer as a consequence of modernity: the 'disunited man . . . ought to harmonize nature and culture within himself' (ibid.: para. 16). Picturing the psyche as comprising 'all kinds of opposites', Jung singled out the spiritual versus instinctual as the counter-positions which 'form the twin poles of that psychic one-sidedness which is typical of the normal man of today':

> Psychic processes therefore behave like a scale along which consciousness 'slides.' At one moment it finds itself in the vicinity of instinct, and falls under its influence; at another, it slides along to the other end where spirit predominates and even assimilates the instinctual processes most opposed to it.
>
> (1954, CW 8: para. 408)

It is tempting to say that multivoicedness is the counterpart postmodern condition. However, it would be more accurate to say that *talk* of multivoicedness – along with words like voice, dialogue, discourse and narrative

– became fashionable in the late twentieth century. Hermans' dissemination of the dialogical-self model is informed by the 'new paradigm' rhetoric that assigns the fallacious belief in a unified Cartesian subject to all old psychologies. A ghost of the Cartesian subject indeed haunted the ψ disciplines, but it was often construed as a source of intellectual tension, not as a 'fact' of human nature. This problematic induced various theories and psychotherapeutic practices based on the recognition of inner disunity as a psychological fact. It was Freud who helped us to 'take seriously the possibility that there is no central faculty, no central self', according to Rorty (1989: 33). It would be more accurate to say that self-integration is a post-Enlightenment cultural ideal, associated with the pathologizing of failures to attain it. That goal is challenged by some postmodernist intellectuals – but seldom by psychotherapists (such as Hermans).

To convey his idea of multivoicedness, Hermans used the analogy of the 'polyphonic' novel as described by Bakhtin in *Problems of Dostoevsky's Poetics*. In such a novel, the plot is told through the intermeshed consciousnesses of different characters. It should be noted that Hermans consulted the 1973 English translation of Bakhtin's 1929 edition of the monograph (an allegedly flawed translation, now out of print). Bakhtin himself substantially revised this monograph in 1963. Although the themes reviewed by Hermans and Kempen are found also in Bakhtin's later revision, some of the nuances to which I point might not be apparent in the earlier version. Ironically, Bakhtin (1984[1963]) attributes invention of the polyphonic novel as an art form to the same nineteenth-century modern condition that gave rise to Jungian and depth psychology in general. The polyphonic novel could be 'realized only in the capitalist era' (ibid.: 19) – speaking of that epoch in the past tense, for Bakhtin was writing under the Soviet regime. 'The multi-leveledness and contradictoriness of social reality was presented as an objective fact of the epoch' (ibid.: 27). Contesting another critic's interpretation of Dostoevsky as based on Hegel, Bakhtin submits that each of Dostoevsky's novels 'presents an opposition, which is never cancelled out dialectically, of many consciousnesses, and they do not merge in the unity of an evolving spirit' (ibid.: 26). Dostoevsky found 'multivoicedness and contradictions not in the spirit, but in the objective social world', where there were '*opposing camps*, and the contradictory relationships among them were not the . . . course of an individual personality, but the *condition of society*' (ibid.: 27). Bakhtin cautions that to speak of a novel as characterized by polyphony is 'a graphic analogy, nothing more': 'It should not be forgotten . . . that the term [polyphony] has its origin in metaphor' (ibid.: 22). Likening the self to such a novel is a metaphor of a metaphor.

The metaphor-of-a-metaphor works on at least two levels in Hermans' theory building. On its surface, it is a convenient picture (albeit one that requires us to learn what a polyphonic novel is before we 'get the picture').

On a deeper level, the analogy focalizes a philosophical position – namely, the dialogical nature of human consciousness – that is correctly attributed to Bakhtin. But in the extrapolation from literary criticism into psychology, there is a subtle slippage of meaning. Bakhtin says: 'In Dostoevsky, consciousness never gravitates toward itself but is always found in intense relationship with another consciousness' (ibid.: 32). Hermans and Kempen say: 'In Bakhtin's (1929/1973) dialogical view, "Consciousness is never self-sufficient; it always finds itself in an intense relationship with another consciousness"' (1993: 41). The conversion of what Bakhtin said about Dostoevsky to a statement about his own view means that certain aspects of Bakhtin's thesis are lost from sight. It is not mistaken about Bakhtin's view, though. In notes made in 1961 towards revising *Dostoevsky's Poetics* (appended to the 1984 translation), Bakhtin ponders the dialogical nature of consciousness: 'To live means to participate in dialogue: to ask questions, to heed, to respond, to agree, and so forth' (ibid.: 293). He uses the metaphor (or metonymy) of voice: the definition of *voice* includes 'a person's worldview and fate. A person enters into dialogue as an integral voice. He participates in it not only with his thoughts, but with his fate and with his entire individuality' (ibid.: 293). However, whilst asserting, 'In actuality a person exists in the forms of *I* and *another*', Bakhtin distinguishes the psychological subject from the protagonist of a story: 'Literature creates utterly specific images of people, where *I* and *another* are combined in a special and unpredictable way . . . This is not a concept of a person' (ibid.: 293–4). He observes that there is 'no causality in Dostoevsky's novels, no genesis, no explanations based on the past, on the influences of the environment or of upbringing, and so forth' (ibid.: 29). In sum, missing is precisely that which narrative scholars regard as fundamental for having a self: personal history and a life story.

The conclusion towards which Bakhtin labours is that 'the thinking human consciousness and the dialogic sphere in which this consciousness exists . . . cannot be reached through a monologic artistic approach' (ibid.: 271). His point is that the polyphonic novel is an *art form* in mimesis with a social reality. He meticulously distinguishes the artistic from the realistic, identifying Dostoevsky's genius in creative violations of realistic documentation of life. Moreover, a literary creation has a creator, and Bakhtin does not let us lose sight of Dostoevsky's authorial role: 'Dostoevsky seeks words and plot situations that provoke, tease, extort, dialogize. In this lies the profound originality of Dostoevsky's creative process' (ibid.: 39). He attributes the frequent occurrence of paired characters in Dostoevsky's work to the novelist's 'stubborn urge to see everything as co-existing', noting that Dostoevsky's fundamental mode is 'not evolution but *coexistence* and *interaction*', expressed as the 'spatiality' of his novels (ibid.: 28; original emphasis). There seems to be a similar stubborn urge in Hermans' theorizing about the dialogical self.

Hermans and Kempen present the dialogical self as an effort to 'combine and integrate two concepts, self and dialogue' (1993: 146). Their premise is that both self and dialogue are characterized by two basic components. On the one side, there is 'the independence and closeness of positions'; on the other, 'their interdependence and openness' (ibid.: 146). They note that this duality has long been applied in descriptions of personality, famously Bakan's agency/communion duality and some other similar ideas, culminating with Hermans' S and O motives. Jung's distinction between 'love' or Eros (in the Freudian sense) and the 'will to power' (Nietzsche and Adler) (see Jung, 1921, CW 6) could be added to their list. Hermans and Kempen submit that S/O duality is 'highly similar to the two defining characteristics of . . . dialogue: dominance and intersubjective exchange' (1993: 147). That is, taking one's turn in a conversation places the speaker in the dominant position, but an intersubjective exchange requires both parties to be open to each other. To be finicky, it could be quipped that anything perceivable involves a similar duality. A foreground shape is seen by virtue of a background against which it stands out, but we wouldn't usually say that the relation of the shape to its surroundings is like a dialogue. Surely there is another reason why the analogy between the self and a dialogue does feel right, why this picture takes us in so powerfully. It could be because *dialogue* already implies *self* by assuming two consciousnesses in communion with each other. Ironically, it is Bakhtin who indirectly aids a deconstruction of any simplistic analogy between self and dialogue. As seen in Chapter 2, Bakhtin defined *utterance* as a unit of communication that has definite boundaries by virtue of being a response to something else and being responded to in turn. It is thus both discrete and inseparable from the flow of communication in which it is embedded. But such flow is an abstraction, separate from any particular speaker and listener, and does not require an assumption of interlocutors' dominance versus mutual openness. It does not require an actual exchange between two people (Bakhtin lists 'scientific treatises' amongst examples of utterances). It does not even require the production of a spoken sentence. Bakhtin was at pains to explain that a silence can also be an utterance if it is a definite response to something and is followed by some definite response. Indeed, silence could be used to position oneself as dominant, e.g. refusing to answer someone of a 'lower' status. In certain situations, it is the listener who is dominant. A policeman interrogating a suspect has powers to demand that the other speaks, and, by complying, the speaker is positioned as subordinate. But such concrete considerations are aspects of what I've proposed to call the dialogic dimension, and have not entered the assumptions of Hermans' dialogical self.

The picture at the core of Hermans' dialogical self comes into sharper focus in a recent analogy supplied by him. 'In a sense the dialogical self is a "society of mind" because there is no essential difference between the positions a person takes as part of the self and the positions people take as members of a heterogeneous society' (Hermans, 2002: 147). Hermans notes that in the sixteenth century Montaigne already alluded to something similar. The idea of isomorphism between self and society is far older. Plato exploits it in *Republic*, in which Socrates debates about the nature of the personality by drawing an analogy with the ideal *polis*. The Platonic analogy rests on an ideal of a society where the incumbents of various roles (guardians, philosophers, etc.) fulfil their differentiated functions towards the harmonious running of the whole. Likewise within the ideal personality, all parts ought to be balanced in relation to each other. In contrast, Hermans' analogy alludes to a realistic modern society. Because a real society does not consist of paired opposites, this analogy does not compel us to assume that any particular I-position is necessarily paired with an opposite – and throws askew the Heraclitean notion of opposites that Hermans sometimes cited (e.g. 1993).

Heraclitus' work has survived only as fragments in the form of quotations by other ancients (e.g. Sweet, 1995). In Plato's *Symposium*, Heraclitus is accredited at length with the idea of conflict as opposition necessary for unity – like day and night, light and shadow, hot and cold – rather than as discord in need of resolution (more on that in the next chapter). Aristotle quotes Heraclitus: 'What is in opposition is in agreement, and the most beautiful harmony comes out of things in conflict (and all happens according to [is born from] strife)' (*Ethics* 1.1155b.4; see also Sweet, 1995: fr. 8). Jung attributed to 'Old Heraclitus, who was indeed a very great sage' the discovery of the 'most marvellous of all psychological laws: the regulative function of opposites', called *enantiodromia*, meaning that 'sooner or later everything runs into its opposite' (1943, CW 7: para. 111). Paired opposites such as day and night never transcend their eternal necessary opposition. 'The one in conflict with itself is held together, like the harmony of the bow and of the lyre' (Heraclitus, quoted in Plato, *Republic*, 1993: 187a; cf. Sweet, 1995: fr. 51). Day and night are united in the harmony of the diurnal cycle, each forever running into its opposite. In contrast, people interlocked in conflict can reconcile their differences by fostering a different outlook on things. Which is the best way to view someone's contradictory I-positions? It is perhaps best to leave it as a matter for a practitioner's judgement regarding particular clients, rather than as a theoretical question about the 'objective' nature of the self.

On deep metaphors

Dialogue serves Hermans as a 'root' metaphor analogy for the self (cf. Sarbin, 1986, and Chapter 3). But the possibility of hitting upon this analogy arises within an already emergent worldview, which incorporated the reference to dialogue into its ontological claims about the self. Jung's picture of the psyche – on which the remainder of the chapter will focus – was made possible by nineteenth-century psychophysical parallelism, which most psychologists and physiologists endorsed well into the twentieth century, viewing it as a scientifically respectable doctrine that allowed psychology to coexist autonomously alongside physiology and other sciences (Heidelberger, 2003). It enters Jung's explicit analogy of psyche and body: 'Just as the human body represents a whole museum of organs, with a long evolutionary history behind them, so we should expect the mind to be organized in a similar way' (1961, CW 18: para. 522). In other words, just as anatomies evolve when more sophisticated structures are added onto primitive ones, the older remaining functional in the living organism, so there must be living fossil structures in the psyche. In a 1925 seminar, Jung spoke allegorically of the 'geology of personality' and provided a sketch depicting a row of volcanic islands rising from the sea (1989[1926]: 133). The summit represents the individual person. The body of the mountain is the family. Below sea-level are geological strata representing, in descending order, 'the clan which unites several families, then the nation which unites still a bigger group' and so forth, through ethnic groups to primate ancestors and 'animal ancestors in general' (ibid.: 133). Below it all there is the 'central fire, with which . . . we are still connected' (ibid.: 134). On this geological scale, human history and personal biography become minuscule and trivial. That which fires the human soul is deep down in Nature.

Jung's vision fired many souls. But picturing the family, clans and nations as residual structures within the island-like person detracts from construing families, etc., as nested social systems in the here-and-now of someone's life – a position that Hermans implicitly conveys in his view of the self as socially extended. To Jung, someone's social context is but the milieu into which the person must adapt, like a tree growing into its locale, its actual development shaped by local constraints and opportunities for fulfilling its ideal form. From the social or dialogical viewpoint, the social context is the surrounding by virtue of which the surrounded can exist at all. Theirs are very different statements of what 'being human' means. To Foucault (1989[1969]), a statement is a group of signs that creates the possibility of a subject, *someone* who enunciates it. Saying that the Jungian model is a 'statement' about the nature of the psyche is more than identifying it as a set of ideas stated by a certain man who once lived. It means hearing an authorial voice in those discursive formations, and either assigning or denying Jung the power to tell us how the psyche behaves. The same applies to Hermans' statement of the dialogical self. Whether we agree or disagree with what Jung or Hermans say may depend on the resonances of the poetic images implicit in their discursive formations.

Their deadlocks of perspective are reflected in differences of the 'deep' metaphors arising from Jung's and Hermans' writings respectively. A deep metaphor – as I propose to use the phrase – is a kaleidoscopic image implied by a particular combination of overlaying concrete analogies deployed by exponents of a theory. It is contingent on specific discursive formations, and therefore continuously changes (because theories are updated with fresh analogies). The idea of a deep metaphor differs from Sarbin's 'root' metaphor. As seen in the previous chapter, Sarbin took from Pepper the description of a linear process leading from a commonsense analogy to its crystallization as the structuring core for a metaphysical system. That description allowed him to make a sharp segregation of worldviews in psychology (imagine trees growing from their separate root systems) – a rhetorical manoeuvre whereby narrative psychology was positioned as the antithesis of psychologies based on metaphors of machine and organism. Whereas Hermans bases his approach in the narrative root-metaphor, and Jung's approach could be attributed to that of the organism, the deep metaphors that emerge from their tropes are somewhat different. In Hermans' case, it is *voice*; in Jung's case, *image*. Image has the connotations of mirror-reflection and likeness. It implies a perceiver who is united with the perceived in a duality of eternal opposition. It implies visibility, and embodies a metaphor of *spatiality*, which implies the (impossible) possibility of seeing the array of intrapsychic contents in its entirety. In contrast, voice connotes a speaker, implying a social agent and authorial position. It implies the articulable as opposed to the visible, and embodies the metaphor of *spatiality*, implying the (impossible) possibility of reading the entire text of a self. Boundaries are shifty, and deep metaphors blur into each other.

'The cave under Jung's house'

One night in 1909, travelling with Freud back from their trip to Clark University in Massachusetts, Jung dreamed of a house where each floor belonged to a different historical era, down to a prehistoric cave-like cellar. When Jung reflected on the house dream from a biographical distance – publicly speaking about it for the first time in the 1925 seminar – he identified it as a milestone in the development of his thought. A notion that he discovered the collective unconscious in this dream has entered the mythology of Jungianism. In 1952, Jung declared in a conversation: 'It was then, at that moment, I got the idea of the collective unconscious' (Bennet, 1985: 36). However, in the specific conversational context, 'that moment' refers – not to the dream as such – but to his rejection of Freud's interpretation of the dream. The significance of the dream for Jung cannot be untangled from his relationship with Freud. In *Memories, Dreams, Reflections*, the dream is told in a chapter entitled 'Sigmund Freud' (Jung, 1963). The subtext of the autobiographical narrative is that the dream showed him how to understand the psyche better than Freud did. That is its dialogic dimension. Its symbolic dimension is stretched out in time: 'a symbol is always more than we can understand at first sight'; the 'symbol does not disguise, it reveals in time' (Jung, 1961, CW 18: paras. 482, 483). Jung hardly woke up suddenly knowing about the collective unconscious. He told Bennet (1983: 74) that he continued to reflect on the dream on and off for months, even years, before it occurred to him that the house represents 'stages of culture'. Nor was the dream image without history:

> In those times I had no idea of the collective unconscious. I thought of the conscious as of a room above, with the unconscious as a cellar underneath and then the earth wellspring, that is, the body, sending up the instincts. . . . That is the figure I had always used for myself, and then came this dream . . .
>
> (Jung, 1989[1926]: 22–3)

In other words, the picture was there before the dream. Partial forerunners of Jung's theory can be found in the nineteenth-century discourses of the unconscious, evolution and land-myth-and-*Volk* (see Chapter 3). But the significance of the dream as a focal point should not be underestimated. Upon reflection, it became an image through which 'a thousand connections are forged by one stroke', to paraphrase Cassirer (1946[1925]: 28). Cassirer goes on to say, 'it is not so much the contemplation of particulars as an awareness of such relationships that constitutes the peculiar historicity, or what we call the historical significance of facts' (ibid.: 28).

Published accounts of the dream reveal that the dream-image continued to evolve in the telling and retelling, like an oral folktale. The morphology of the dream account raises the question of which is the most reliable version. The version that is usually cited appears in *Memories, Dreams, Reflections* (henceforth MDR). Its fidelity to what Jung actually dreamed is dubious, though I shall argue that it is the most illuminating regarding its function as a symbol for Jung. It is the narrative image through which those thousand connections are forged by one stroke. Although the chapter in which it appears was partially written by Jaffé, who incorporated into it parts from the 1925 seminar, the dream version seems authentic insofar as it was told by Jung towards the end of his life. It does not match the version of the dream that he told in the 1925 seminar, but instead accords with what Jung told Bennet in 1951 and again in 1952 (Bennet, 1983, 1985). In the MDR version, all the elements cohere into a perfect whole. The 1925 version is less neat, indeed more like a dream. The MDR and Bennet versions correspond closely to an analogy that Jung provided – without mentioning the dream – in 'Mind and earth', first published in 1927 and revised in 1931 with no alterations to the relevant part. Doing away with the obligation to be faithful to the 'facts' of the dream in that essay freed him to reconstruct the picture in the service of his theory. It seems plausible that when he retold the dream to Bennet and Jaffé three decades later, his earlier imaginative analogy became fused with the actual dream in his memory.

In 'Mind and Earth', Jung takes us on an imaginary descent through a building 'whose upper storey was erected in the nineteenth century, the ground-floor dates back to the sixteenth century' and its masonry was 'reconstructed from a tower built in the eleventh century' (1931, CW 10: para. 54). The cellar reveals Roman foundations, and under it there is a cave. He sums up, 'That would be the picture of our psychic structure' (ibid.: para. 54). In the 1925 seminar, he told that he dreamed of a 'medieval . . . big, complicated house with many rooms, passages, and stairways' (1989[1926]: 23). He comes in from the street and directly goes down to a vaulted Gothic room, from there into a cellar, where he finds a square hole. With a lantern in hand he peeps down and sees 'dusty stairs, very much worn' which lead him to another cellar, 'this one of very ancient structure, perhaps Roman' (ibid.: 23). There is a hole in the floor, and through it he looks down into 'a tomb filled with prehistoric pottery, bones, and skulls' (ibid.: 23). Certain details – coming in from the street, the lantern – did not survive into later accounts. Other details were added. There is no mention of an upper floor in 1925, yet later he would find himself there. The MDR version opens:

> I was in a house I did not know, which had two storeys. It was 'my house.' I found myself in the upper storey, where there was a kind of salon furnished with fine old pieces in rococo style. On the walls hung a number of precious old paintings. I wondered that this should be my house, and thought, 'Not bad.' But then it occurred to me that I did not know what the lower floor looked like. Descending the stairs, I reached the ground floor.
>
> (Jung, 1963: 155)

In all versions, he discovers a lower level under a cellar dated to Roman times. In 1925 Jung told the seminar audience that he looked down into a tomb-like space and, since the dust was undisturbed, he thought that he had made a great discovery. He told something similar to Bennet in 1951. Only in MDR he seems to enter it:

> I saw a stairway of narrow stone steps leading down into the depths. These, too, I descended, and entered a low cave cut into the rock. Thick dust lay on the floor, and in the dust were scattered bones and broken pottery, like remains of a primitive culture. I discovered two human skulls, obviously very old and half disintegrated. Then I awoke.
>
> (Ibid.: 155)

Jung's sense of belonging in the house intensified over the years. Whereas in 1925, it is a house entered from the street, later it is a house inside which he is already present. In 1951 he told the dream to Bennet more or less as in MDR; but upon reading Bennet's manuscript in 1961, Jung added the words 'in *my* house', remarking that this was important because it showed his identification with the house (Bennet, 1983: 73n.). In 1959, Jung associated it with his uncle's 'very old house in Basel which was built in the old moat of the town and had two cellars; the lower one was very dark and like a cave' (Bennet, 1985: 118). In 1961, Jung provided Bennet with further information about his uncle's house. It was the priest's house at Basel Cathedral. In 1960, excavations were carried out there and it was found that the house was built on Roman remains, and underneath was a cellar like that in the dream. 'This interested him very much – that somehow it was in the family' (ibid.: 124). His identification with the dream culminates in *Man and His Symbols*, where the dream is described as a short summary of his life (Jung, 1964).

All versions of the dream as told by Jung and others centre on the descent through the stratified house to its prehistoric lowest level, highlighting the idea of the psyche as evolving over an immensely long time. A two-storey house is surely an understatement, to say the least. In a revealing embellishment, Stein (1998) describes how Jung finds himself in a house of 'many' levels. He goes down to 'the basement (the recent historical past) and beyond that down through several sub-cellars (the ancient historical past, like the Greek and Roman, and finally into the prehistoric and Palaeolithic past)' (ibid.: 89). Jung mentions only a few specific periods – and, as will be seen, their specification is important for the allegory of the dream. Usually, the descent is implicitly taken as depicting the continuity of the psyche's evolution. In MDR, the continuity of the cave with the house is captured in imagery of thick dust on its floor and scattered broken pottery, which give the place a domestic feel. In other versions, the lower cellar is like a tomb. The precise wording might seem trivial, but it is poetically crucial. A poet would not choose the simile lightly. A tomb or grave is manmade, a mark of civilization, unlike a cave. Jung's description of the cave in 'Mind and Earth' – where the analogy was liberated from the dream – implicitly conveys its discontinuity from the building. Historical periods become geological strata once we enter 'a choked-up cave with Neolithic tools in the upper layer and remnants of fauna from the same period in the lower layers' (1931, CW 10: para. 54). Jung probably had in mind the Palaeolithic era. The anachronistic reference to Neolithic tools appears in Hull's translation, but is absent in both the German original and the Baynes translation of the 1927 version. In those, there is 'under the cellar a filled-in cave, in the floor of which stone tools are found and remnants of glacial fauna in the layers below' (Jung, 1927: 119). *Glacial* indicates Palaeolithic. Yet pottery – seen in the dream as told in MDR –

first appeared in the Neolithic era. Neolithic tombs are megalithic constructions of impressive engineering, which seems a far cry from what Jung associates with the cave:

> [Here] we reach the naked bed-rock, and with it that prehistoric time when reindeer hunters fought for a bare and wretched existence against the elemental forces of wild nature. The men of that age were still in full possession of their animal instincts, without which life would have been impossible.
>
> (Ibid.: para. 55)

When distilling a poetic image from the dream, Jung took the imaginary descent as far back in human time as imaginable, placing the collective unconscious in our remotest past.

The dream, especially as told in MDR, communicates Jung's crisis of confidence in Freud around 1909, but this perfect narrative took decades to mature. Perhaps when Jung could no longer recall the dream exactly as it was, this was how he felt the dream ought to be, like a poet who finally got the rhyme right. Freud and Jung alike saw the instinctual as being expressed in the cultural. In the dream as Jung told it late in life (and earlier in 'Mind and Earth'), the house with its three principal levels has a striking resemblance to Freud's model of the psyche with its id, ego and superego – as if Jung took Freud's blueprint and turned it upside down. Freudian theory assumes an ascent from the primordial id to the socialized superego. The movement is reversed in Jung's dream action (he descends). Jung's great discovery – the resolution of his crisis – lay in the descent to the cave. But the heuristic potential of the image as a picture of the psyche required a representation of modern consciousness with which to contrast the prehistoric unconscious. Whatever Jung really dreamed, such representation was not yet present in the 1925 account. A couple of years later it was supplied in 'Mind and Earth', where Jung explicitly likens an upper floor to consciousness. Much later, the upper floor enters the dream too, now complete with a salon furnished with fine old pieces and precious old paintings, like a bourgeois salon where Freud has us live in our civilized moralistic conscious state. However, the tripartite structure as such is not germane for Jung's theory (or dream). More important is the bipolarity of consciousness and the unconscious, given in the symmetry of above and below.

Above, there is the house, a monument of civilization. The specific historical periods stated in MDR are not trivial. Why is the top floor Rococo? He says that the salon had an antiquated appearance, though a comfortable lived-in atmosphere (talking with Bennet, Jung likened it to his own study), and there are precious things there. Yet the ornamental and frivolous Rococo style is an apt representation for Jung's attitude to modern consciousness – the superficial, veneer-like, aspect of the psyche. Why is the basement Roman? In the upper floor he notices the removable furnishings, but in the basement he closely examines the walls and floor. The classical world is the foundations for modern European consciousness. The whole house is well ordered. Each floor has its own theme, and they are arranged logically in descending order. The house is infused with the aesthetic of classicism: simplicity of form and proportion. It accords with structuralism, which 'above all insists upon preserving the coherence and completion of each totality . . . [and] prohibits the consideration of that which is incomplete or missing' (Derrida, 1978[1967]: 26). It is consistent with the ideal of science: order and balance, elegance and parsimony of explanation. It is the safe house of rationality.

Below, there is the cave, an existence within nature, within the earth. In the imaginary journey in 'Mind and Earth' Jung tells us, 'the deeper we descend into the house . . . the more we find ourselves in the darkness, till finally we reach . . . that prehistoric time when reindeer hunters fought for a bare and wretched existence' (1931, CW 10: para. 55). Here romanticism is in full swing, with its aesthetic of strong emotion, rebellion and freedom from classical form. In the poetic image of the dream, the cave connotes wilderness at the dawn of time. It is womb-like, the place of existence before the birth of the self into the house that History and Culture built. According to Jung (1989[1926]: 47), the motif of a cave is 'an archetype of considerable power . . . for the mystery attaching to caves comes down from immemorial time'. It is listed among mythological motifs of 'big' dreams that characterize the hero's journey and represent 'all things that in no way touch the banalities of everyday . . . the process of becoming' (Jung, 1948c, CW 8: para. 558). This could explain the importance of the cave in Jung's own dream; or, conversely, the personal significance of 'his' cave might explain why he interpreted the motif elsewhere as he did (or both). A cave is associated with descent. Jung notes that the 'purpose of the descent as universally exemplified in the myth of the hero is to show that only in the region of danger (watery abyss, cavern, forest, island, castle, etc.) can one find the "treasure hard to attain"' (1944, CW 12: para. 438). Reporting a patient's dream, in which two boys are in a cave and a third falls in as if through a pipe, Jung suggests that the cave represents 'the darkness and seclusion of the unconscious; the two boys correspond to the two unconscious functions' (ibid.: para. 197). The dream has a parallel with Jung's own (MDR), where he too 'falls' into a cave inhabited by two (skulls). Regarding another patient's dream, in which the dreamer is *'wandering about in a dark cave, where a battle is going on between good and evil'* (original emphasis), Jung suggests that the 'dark cave corresponds to the vessel containing the warring opposites. The self is made manifest in the opposites and in the conflict between them. . . . Hence the way to the self begins with conflict' (ibid.: paras. 258–9). Although in Jung's dream there is no apparent danger in the cave under the house, he was at the time in a 'region of danger' (his situation with Freud), and the dream descent, where he found 'treasure hard to attain', marked a way to the self.

In the MDR version, he finds a pair of skulls. In other versions, this element is sometimes omitted or becomes 'bones', 'skeletons', 'many skulls' or just 'skulls'. The skulls are played down in Jungian accounts of the dream, but Freud regarded them as the key to understanding it. There is a history. In Bremen, on the eve of sailing to the USA, Jung became keenly interested in a discovery of mummified corpses in the peat bogs of Northern Germany. He recalled that this 'got on Freud's nerves. "Why are you so concerned with these corpses?" he asked me several times' (Jung, 1963: 153). During one such conversation Freud fainted, and later told Jung that he was convinced that 'all this chatter about corpses' meant that Jung had death wishes towards him (ibid.: 153). Not surprisingly, Freud was perturbed by the skulls in Jung's dream on the return journey, and pressed Jung to reveal whom he was wishing death upon. That interpretation never felt right to Jung. In a way, Freud was right: the house dream quickened the death of Freudian theory for Jung and sealed their acrimonious separation. In 'Mind and Earth', Jung does not mention skulls (there is only 'fauna', which could be human but he doesn't say so). Yet the skulls seem foremost at the back of his mind even there, when he apologizes for the 'lame analogy' on grounds that 'in the psyche there is nothing that is just a dead relic. Everything is alive' (1931, CW 10: para. 55). It is as if he still conducts an internal dialogue with Freud:

'Why are you so concerned with these corpses?' asked Freud in 1909.
'Because in the psyche nothing is just a dead relic,' Jung replied in 1927.

The skulls are silent (there's no reason why skulls can't speak in dreams), and their muteness is pregnant with meanings. They are not inert remains, not dead relics. On the contrary, those fragile, half-disintegrated skulls are very vibrant, very alive, for Jung. He wakes up as soon as he discovers them.

The skulls as specified in the MDR are important precisely because they are human and a pair. They constitute an indivisible unity, the ancestral mother and father, alive in each of us in the masculine and feminine duality of the Jungian psyche. The duality of the dreamer (one) and skulls (two) could be amplified with the Chinese yin–yang concept (which Jung mentions in 'Mind and Earth', though not in connection with the house analogy). The masculine principle (yang) is represented in the *I Ching* with a solid line standing for the creative, light giving, active and strong, and is associated with the image of heaven. The feminine principle (yin) is represented with a broken line for the 'dark, yielding, receptive primal power of the yin . . . its image is the earth' (Wilhelm, 1950: 10). In the house dream – which ought to be renamed the cave dream – the dreamer is self-aware, active, following at will a solid line of descent from the light above. The skulls are a divided unit, like the broken line, unaware, passive, their silence resounding with the dark, yielding, receptive power of the earth. In the whole house there is not another soul. And down here in the cave, in a place that is deep inside the house and simultaneously outside it, two human skulls forever hold their secret. Here is the dark mystery of existence that could never be fully brought to the light of consciousness, hinting at the unknowable distant past and anticipating the likewise unknown future. Here is the incomplete, the missing, the uncertainties that structuralism cannot tolerate. Here Jung finds his way.

Chapter 5

The ebb and flow of 'psychic energy'

Silent and void
It stands alone and does not change,
Goes around and does not weary.
It is capable of being the mother of the world.
I know not its name
So I style it 'the way'.

(Lao Tzu, 1963: 82)

Whether energy is God or God is energy concerns me very little, for how, in any case, can I know such things? But to give appropriate psychological explanations – this I must be able to do.

(Jung, 1931a, CW 8: para. 678)

Concluding this book with a review of Jung's concept of psychic energy is apt for several reasons. It is central to Jung's description of symbol formation, though neglected in contemporary Jungian studies, and Jung himself stopped developing the concept after the 1920s. His 'final word' in that regard is a 1928 essay, 'On psychic energy' (CW 8). From 1912 onwards, Jung presented his concept as an amendment of Freud's theory, though it is radically different:

By libido I mean *psychic energy*. Psychic energy is the *intensity* of a psychic process, its *psychological value*. This does not imply an assignment of value, whether moral, aesthetic, or intellectual; the psychological value is already implicit in its *determining* power, which expresses itself in definite psychic effects. Neither do I understand libido as a psychic *force*, a misconception that has led many critics astray.

(Jung, 1921, CW 6: para. 778; original emphasis)

We shouldn't be misled by the linearity of terminological succession. *Psychological value* is not a synonym for Freud's *libido*, but its antonym: 'Value requires for its explanation a quantitative concept, and a qualitative concept like sexuality can never serve as a substitute' (1928, CW 8: para. 51). Echoing Schopenhauer's distinction between Ideas and Will – that is, phenomena (or their representations) and the dynamic lawfulness of their interrelationships – Jung differentiates between the two concepts: 'A qualitative concept is always the description of a thing, a substance; whereas a quantitative concept deals with relations of intensity and never with a substance or a thing' (ibid.: para. 51). His quantitative concept (which doesn't involve quantification) refers to the relative affective implications of different elements of experience, by virtue of which those elements are experienced as differing in their significance. There is no equivalent concept in postmodern psychology (another reason for reviewing Jung's concept). At the interface between psychotherapy and postmodern psychology, Hermans' concept of valuations concerns the emotional intensity and direction of narrative self-description, as seen in Chapter 4. But it remains a descriptive concept, at bottom a practical tool for quantifying clients' self-evaluations. At the 'soft' edge of academic postmodern psychology, the narrative approach concerns how people make their experiences meaningful by means of stories, as seen in Chapter 3. But the question of meaning is construed as inviting the identification of which stories are meaningful to whom, as opposed to asking why some stories and not others become meaningful. At its most radical, postmodern psychology redefines the psychological subject as a position opening up in the flow of discourse, as seen in Chapter 2. We may speak of our embodied embedding in the whole flow, to paraphrase Shotter; but 'the way in which our immediate, bodily reactions *necessarily relate* us to our surroundings, has remained *rationally invisible* to us' (Shotter, 1998: 34; original emphasis). This is the dilemma of postmodern psychology as a *psychology* (see Bayer and Shotter, 1998; Nightingale and Cromby, 1999). Jung's 'psychic energy' is not the answer (I don't know what is), but it can help to bring the question into focus in the manner of triangulation. That's a third reason for reviewing it. A fourth and chief reason is that the whole apparatus of symbol formation described by Jung comes into play when he tries to say what he means by 'psychic energy'.

In terms of psychological theories, Jung's conception has a close family resemblance – not to the Freudian libido – but to a view associated with Gestalt theory around the 1920s, articulated notably by Kurt Lewin (1935; Jones, 2001, 2002c, and below). Lewin's field theory is a direct precursor of ecological systems theories that emerged in psychology during the 1960s and 1970s, though their exponents don't refer to energy (Lewin did). By the time that it became fashionable to speak of ecological systems, talk of mental energy was hardly heard any more.

A similar trajectory could be traced through the literature of analytical psychology. In 1948, Esther Harding published her book *Psychic Energy*, prefaced by Jung, which went into a second edition in 1963. It is a *tour de force* of symbols and their signification – and contains no actual definition of psychic energy. The term was used in a matter-of-fact way. By the 1980s, Andrew Samuels asked whether analytical psychology needs a concept of energy at all, though he conceded that 'the notion of energy, even if taken nowadays purely as a metaphor, helps to explain differences in perception' (1985: 114). For sure, it continues to be acknowledged in textbooks as something that Jung said. Stein (1998) devotes a whole chapter of his textbook to it. Sporadic scholarly studies seek to clarify Jung's meaning (Tresan, 2004), identify his intellectual sources (Shamdasani, 2003) or uncover conceptual parallels, e.g. with Deleuze (Kerslake, 2004) or Lewin (Jones, 2001). Those may offer fresh insights into what Jung was saying, but there is no engagement on a par with the current engagement with arche-types, no ongoing discussions about its clinical application, in the main publications of analytical psychology. Some analysts reinterpret Jungian ideas, especially archetypes, by reference to dynamic systems (Saunders and Skar, 2001; McDowell, 2001; Hogenson, 2006), but don't discuss psychic energy – just as systems approaches developed in social and developmental psychology three or four decades ago have no use for the energy metaphor. Like all utterances, the term 'energy' is characterized by what Bakhtin called heteroglossia; that is, its meaning is contingent on the specific conditions under which it is uttered.

Since at least the 1960s, mostly outside academic discourses, Jung's original concept became eclipsed by Western extrapolations from Oriental mysticism. Notions of an intrinsic energy of the universe that flows through mind and body are common throughout the East – but such a notion is absent in Jung's theorizing about psychic energy and is incommensurable with his idea of psychological value. His revision of Freud's libido was meant to inform psychological inquiries, and whether 'energy is God or God is energy' concerned him very little. Likewise, the present critique considers the concept in the context of epistemological positions in modern psychology, to start with. My position is that the explanatory utility of the energy metaphor is highly debatable. To make a stronger claim than Samuels, Jung's metaphor does not even help to explain differences in perception; it muddles up the explanation. My fascination with this concept stems from its function as a symbol or a poetic image. Identifying how and why it muddles up the explanation can tell us something about the nature of human understanding.

Jung's attempt to define psychic energy confronts the paradox of trying to name the unnameable. In the hermeneutic whole of his psychology, this concept exists in a Heraclitean opposition to ideas like archetypes and complexes. On the one side, there is 'matter': the materiality of the myriad nameable things that constitute human worlds, actual and imaginary. On the other, there is 'energy': a constant inherent in relations of movement, the *way* of things. 'The way that can be spoken of is not the constant way, the name that can be named is not the constant name' (Lao Tzu, 1963: 57). If Jung's concept is understood as a symbol – the best possible expression under the circumstances for something that is divined and not fully understood – we could expect other symbols to come to life in its stead when the circumstances have changed, as in postmodernity. At the same time, ideas and even images have histories. Bergson (1911: 316) commented that ways of thinking developed from Plato onward reveal how the intellect grasps things when regarding 'universal becoming' by means of 'snapshots . . . of its flowing. So that, even today, we shall philosophize in the manner of the Greeks, we shall rediscover, without needing to know them, such and such of their general conclusions.' The picture that took in both Jung and Freud – the 'stream' analogy of libidinal flow – could come into focus by examining Plato and Heraclitus, as discussed towards the chapter's end. Nowadays, if we're 'postmodern', we might not be fired up by the energy metaphor; but we still speak of our embedding in flows.

Machine theory and field dynamics

Just as a dream gets its imagery from what is known through the senses, so Jung's thesis got its ideations from the discourses of his milieu. Its most immediate context is psychoanalytical theory, but Jung recruited various claims that were 'in the air', so as to scaffold his opposition to Freud. The scientific conception of energy was hotly debated by *fin-de-siècle* thinkers in the German world, and some of that spilled over to speculations about mental energy. This was the space of questions within which Jung placed his thesis. Little of that enters the space of questions defining postmodern psychology – except for one perennial controversy, to which Jung linked his revision of Freud's concept. Should psychology seek to identify the causal mechanisms underlying some observed behaviour or seek to understand the behaviour by reference to its function? Jung's departure from Freud involves a switch from the causal-mechanistic to the functional explanation.

The 1928 essay begins with a strict distinction between 'energy' and 'force'. Force implies a causal factor that operates on a pre-existing, otherwise static, structure. The introduction of some force into the system is a definite event that initiates structural transformations. Force is by implication an external factor, something that at one time was not there in the system and later it was. This is in keeping with the conventional view of the libido as that which motivates the psyche. Jung wanted to reserve the term 'energy' for indicating a property of the psyche as a dynamic system. The lawfulness of relations of movement is by definition a property of a structure defined as lawful system in motion. Similarly, Lewin – who wrote at great length about fallacies of causal explanations in psychology – asserted, in italics, that *psychical tensions and energies belong to systems which are in themselves dynamic unities*' (1935: 62). A property of the system should not be mistaken for a causal factor, i.e. something that kicks that system into motion. 'To substitute a qualitative concept for energy is inadmissible. . . . This would be in biology vitalism, in psychology sexualism (Freud)' (Jung, 1928, CW 8: para. 51).

Jung justifies the energy/force distinction by drawing attention to two ways in which physical events are understood, namely the 'causal-mechanistic' viewpoint and the 'energic' or (interchangeably) 'final' viewpoint, submitting that the same distinction applies also to the description of psychic events. The causal-mechanistic view 'conceives an event as the effect of a cause, in the sense that unchanging substances change their relations to one another according to fixed laws' (ibid.: para. 2). In contrast, the energic is 'in essence final; the event is traced back from effect to cause on the assumption that some kind of energy underlies the changes in phenomena' (ibid.: para. 3). This presupposes knowing the outcome, having the full (final?) facts before us. Only with such knowledge could we identify the dynamic interrelations among phenomena and may discover the function of some focal phenomena. It is important to note that Jung's misleadingly named 'principle of finality' is *not* teleological in the sense of an explanation that 'contains the idea of an anticipated end or goal' (ibid.: para. 3, n. 4).

Jung's final or energic view accords with what is called a functional explanation in psychology, though the term has two meanings that are incompatible with each other. In one use, the functional explanation is indeed teleological: 'function' is taken as meaning 'purpose', and the explanation would assume an end-goal towards which the observed behaviour strives. In the other use, 'function' is understood in a mathematical sense, which posits the *likelihood* of some behaviour as the function (outcome) of the interaction between two or more independent variables. Such explanation identifies principles or general laws (whereas the teleological is a reverse causal explanation).

The confusing terminology of the 'final' could be found in Bergson, whose thought has significant parallels with Jung's (Gunter, 1982) and a significant role in Jung's development of his ideas (Shamdasani, 2003). Discussing evolution, Bergson contrasted the mechanistic approach with the 'doctrine of finality, which says that the parts have been brought together on a preconceived plan with a view to a certain end' (1911: 88). He objected to them on grounds that 'both mechanism and finalism [are], at bottom, only standpoints to which the human mind has been led by considering the work of man' (ibid.: 89). In other words, those are based in misleading metaphors. His own doctrine of the 'vital impetus' is difficult to grasp and has been mistaken for 'mechanistic' vitalism. Like finalism, Bergson's philosophy 'represents the organized world as a harmonious whole'; but it admits 'much discord', for species and individuals compete for survival, so much so that harmony 'does not exist in fact; it exists rather in principle' (ibid.: 51). Finalism is seriously mistaken, in Bergson's view, in failing to realize that 'harmony is rather behind us than before us' – only in retrospect we can see how things fits in together to bring about the present situation: 'once the road has been travelled, we can glance over it, mark its direction . . . and speak as there had been pursuit of an end' (ibid.: 51). What Jung calls the 'final' approach is not identical with what Bergson identified as finalism, but he does posit a pre-given harmony of psychic structure and regards its striving towards its own fulfilment as its natural process. It is like the biologically pre-given holistic nature of an individual organism – both products of evolution, according to Jung. Bergson speaks of evolution itself.

To Jung, causal-mechanistic and final or energic explanations are mutually exclusive only as ways of explaining phenomena, as opposed to being rival descriptions of the empirical world. As he put it, 'this intolerable contradiction only comes about through the illegitimate and thoughtless projection into the object of what is a mere point of view' (Jung, 1928, CW 8: para. 5). For example (mine), we can either say that the apple fell down because it became detached from the tree or cite the law of gravity by way of explanation. Clearly, neither explanation rules out the other regarding what really happened. But it would be a mistake to say that the apple fell because the law of gravity 'kicked in' at a particular moment. In drawing the strict distinction between force and energy, Jung did not challenge the legitimacy of postulating causal factors, but drew attention to what he saw as a confusion of the two kinds of explanations. 'The concept of quantity should never be qualitative at the same time, otherwise it would never enable us to expound the relations between forces' (ibid.: paras. 26–7). For example (again mine), thirst impels an animal to seek water; but the energy expressed or, in Jungian jargon, 'invested' in this behaviour would reflect the degree to which thirst is more compelling than fear of predators prowling by the river. The outcome would be a function of the 'quantitative' interrelation in terms of affect – positive/negative, stronger/weaker. We may drop all mention of 'forces' and simply talk about thirst and fear; but the animal's actual behaviour cannot be explained without assuming that the animal perceived different elements of its environment as having different affective intensity and direction in relation to each other.

When Jung was putting the final touches to his revision of libidinal theory, Gestalt psychologists were describing the world-as-perceived in terms of a field surrounding a perceiver. In a chapter entitled 'Dynamics and machine theory', Köhler (1930: 89) objected to behaviourism and introspectionism on the grounds that these wrongly assume that either 'inherited machine arrangements' or 'secondary acquired arrangements' determine what happens in the nervous system. 'These authors never entertain the idea that some specific and orderly function might occur without being controlled either by special arrangements pre-established *ad hoc* or by arrangements acquired in learning' (ibid.: 89). The third alternative is not vitalism, he argued, but a theory that does justice to the dynamics of perceptual experience. The 'machine theory excludes *organization of process* in the field' (ibid.: 96; original emphasis). The idea was extended and applied in social psychology by Kurt Lewin. His concept of the 'life space' builds upon the idea of *Umwelt*, attributed to von Uexküll (early 1900s). *Umwelt* refers to the environment as experienced by an animal: a complex of foods, enemies, means of protection and so forth. Combining that with the idea of 'fields of forces' in physics – newly developed when he was a student in Berlin around 1910 – Lewin postulated life-space forces (*Umweltkräfte*), which are abstract patterns of change, discernible by the effects on behaviour that contact with material and social objects may have. The life space consists of *Aufforderungscharaktere* (literally: invitation characters), translated into English as 'valences'. Valences could be positive or negative, in that certain things (objects, activities) invite either approach or avoidance. This is epitomized in the famous formula: $B = f(P,E)$. It represents behaviour B as the function of the interaction between states of the person P and of environment E at a given moment (e.g. Lewin, 1935: 79).

Jung's thinking about psychic energy unfolds along a line roughly parallel to that which led Lewin to the 'field of forces' idea. There is no indication that Jung knew about Lewin and Lewin did not mention Jung (as far as I'm aware regarding both). Jung had an academic affiliation in Berlin in 1910, but if he knew of the 'field' idea that was developed there at the time he didn't assimilate it into his 1928 essay on psychic energy. Instead, an earlier notion of energy, associated with the 'energetics' movement (Ostwald, Mach, and others), seems echoed in that essay, perhaps hinted at in its original title, *Über die Energetik der Seele*, 'on the energetic of the soul' (a point to which David Tresan drew my attention in personal communications). The energetics movement was embroiled in the idealism versus materialism controversies that raged in the late nineteenth century in the Germanic world, and its claims were discredited by physicists long before 1928. The rise and fall of the energetics movement had little direct bearing on what Jung was trying to say regarding the energy concept in psychology. The thrust of his argument since 1912 was that libido is not the desire of a specific kind (e.g. sexual) but generic, insofar as it is an intensity of interest. It is a concept that 'expands into a conception of intentionality in general ... an energy-value which is able to communicate itself to any field of activity whatsoever, be it power, hunger, hatred, sexuality, or religion, without ever being itself a specific instinct' (1952, CW 5: para. 197).

Jung describes at length the behaviour of birds to make his point. Birds invest energy first in building a nest, then in tending the young. Flying about collecting nesting material consumes the same energy as flying about collecting food for the chicks, though the type and goal of the activity has changed. Jung's analogy of the birds is a heuristic, not a theory about bird behaviour or biology (he is not talking about the caloric energy actually spent in flying for whatever purpose). His examples from nature are analogies meant to give a handle on abstract concepts concerning the psyche. The analogy implies: there might be an instinctual force that motivates the bird to look for nesting materials, and another force motivating it to look for food; but a taxonomy of forces is besides the point. The point is that at any given time there is intense interest in something. In the 1928 essay, Jung's premise posits that symbol formation could be understood by reference to the symbol's function within a system of psychological values – a system whose dynamics are not reducible to specific drives, instincts or desires. He contends that the 'immediate experience of quantitative psychic relations' justifies 'at least a provisional view of the psyche as a relatively closed system' (ibid.: para. 11).

In other words, the psyche could be viewed as a mathematical space that is constituted of correlations among various variables. In the 1950s, independently of both Jung and Lewin, George Kelly operationalized a similar premise in his personal construct psychology. He argued his case for it partly through criticizing the motivational concept of mental energy that was prevalent at the time, which he regarded as redundant: we don't need to conjecture something that kicks the personality into motion, for it is already a system in motion (Kelly, 1963). Jung, Lewin and Kelly alike approach the psychological subject as a dynamic system of psychological values. Lewin's and Kelly's arguments for and against 'energy', respectively, were preludes to offering specific logico-mathematical tools for psychological inquiries. In contrast, Jung's 'quantitative' concept of psychic energy remained submerged in qualitative contemplation of intrapsychic processes. The somewhat longer second half of the 1928 essay is devoted to explaining the formation of symbols by reference to libidinal progression and regression – a metaphor inherited from Freud.

Characteristics of Jung's theorizing

To paraphrase Jung's physiological analogy of the psyche, cited in the previous chapter, just as the body represents a 'whole museum of organs' with a long evolutionary history, so the 1928 thesis represents the organic evolution of his thinking about psychic energy since 1912. That is characteristic of Jung's style. In tackling the task of theorizing psychic energy, he did not wipe the slate clean but tried to improve the picture that Freud already put there. A related characteristic is his faith in the necessity of the concept. Jung did not ask whether we need a concept of libido, but only what is the best way to understand it. His theorizing took off in earnest in the 1912 monograph, but the 'pure' concept of psychic energy as presented in 1928 is not apparent there yet. He left the original claims unaltered when revising the monograph 39 years later for the Swiss edition (becoming CW 5), partly perhaps because he intended it to remain a historical document. It is not incorrect to say that in 1912 Jung proposed to replace Freud's concept of sexual energy with a concept of generic energy; but what he ended up asserting in 1928 is something else again.

Jung's 1912 thesis begins with a practical puzzle: something is amiss with Freud's notion of libido as sexual energy, for it does not seem applicable to dementia praecox. The illness is not associated with heightened sexuality (as Freudian theory would predict, according to Jung), but is characterized instead with the generation of a fantasy world. Jung recognized mythological elements in his patients' fantasies. That discovery set Jung on what is the main thrust of the 1912 monograph and much of his subsequent work, leading to the articulation of archetype theory. Freud did acknowledge instinctual desires of a non-sexual nature; e.g. nutritive. In *Three Essays on Sexuality*, first published in 1905, he distinguished between libidinal and other forms of psychical energy, and asserted that 'the sexual processes occurring in the organism are distinguished from the nutritive processes by a special chemistry' (1953: 217). In a portion added in 1915, in which a reaction to Jung's 1912 thesis could be heard, Freud defines the concept of libido as 'a quantitatively variable force' serving as 'a measure of processes and transformations occurring in the field of sexual excitation' (ibid.: 217). This distinguishes the libido from 'the energy which must be supposed to underlie mental processes in general' and also means that it has 'a *qualitative* character' (ibid.: 217; original emphasis). Revising the *Three Essays* again in 1920, Freud added that although his libidinal theory is incomplete,

> It would, however, be sacrificing all that we have gained hitherto from psychoanalytic observation, if we were to follow the example of C. G. Jung and water down the meaning of the concept of libido by equating it with psychical instinctual force in general. The distinguishing of the sexual instinctual impulses from the rest and the consequent restriction of the concept of libido to the former receives strong support from the assumption . . . that there is a special chemistry of the sexual function.
>
> (Ibid.: 218–19)

Freud sees '"ego-libido" . . . whose production, increase or diminution, distribution and displacement' explain psychosexual phenomena (ibid.: 217). It is accessible to study only when becoming 'object-libido'. As such, we can perceive it concentrating upon objects (i.e. mental representations), fixing upon them, abandoning them, moving from object to object and thus directing sexual activity to satisfaction, 'that is, to the partial and temporary extinction, of the libido' (ibid.: 217).

The Freudian model has it that when the mother (as an internal figure) is the object of sexual desire, the incest taboo intervenes to block the flow of libido, which consequently is diverted elsewhere, e.g. into symbolic substitutes. Jung did not reject outright that narrative of mechanism, but subverted its course by revisiting the question *why* there is the longing for the mother.

> The symbol-creating process substitutes for the mother the city, the well, the cave, the Church, etc. . . . Because the incest taboo opposes the libido and blocks the path to regression, it is possible for the libido to be canalized into mother analogies thrown up by the unconscious. In this way the libido becomes progressive again, and even attains a level of consciousness higher than before.
>
> (Jung, 1952, CW 5: para. 313)

Because 'mother' has simultaneously the strong positive value as a source of shelter and rebirth and the strong negative value as a tabooed sexual object – a case of what Lewin would call an approach/avoidance conflict – there emerges a new content, at a tangent to them both. To Freud, symbols are tokens for unattainable objects, which at most alleviate the inner conflict through a kind of escapism. To Jung, symbols enable 'moving on' from the irresolvable conflict by virtue of introducing something new into the surrounding field (to borrow the language of the Gestalt theorists). Now in the *Umwelt* there are also the mother analogies appearing in dreams, visions, etc. – concrete experiences in their own right, which would have *psychological value*; in Jungian jargon, a numinous quality. Concrete symbolic productions make the psychological significance of something 'visible'. This offsets the dynamics of the field, the balance of forces, so to speak. If, to Freud, symbols are symptoms of some inner pathology, and need not be considered once we diagnose the malaise and address it directly – to Jung, symbols are the 'healthy' and indispensable means for personal development. We need to recognize their significance and work with them.

Some of the confusion about Jung's revision might not have arisen had he coined some new term rather than retain the term libido. However, he did retain it. This blurred the distinctiveness of his thesis compared to Freud's, and has meant that those who read him from a Freudian perspective are likely to mistake his innovation and to regard him as mistaken about the libido. Jung is accused of 'evacuating the libido of all sexual content by associating it exclusively with cultural process', a move that 'leads Jung to stress the essential plasticity of malleability of the libido' (Copjec, 1994: 22). Kristeva (1980: 276) dismisses 'Jung's dead end with its archetypal configurations of libidinal substance taken out of the realm of sexuality'. However, libido as *psychological value* cannot be configured or have properties of malleability and plasticity:

> The idea of energy is not that of substance moved in space, it is a concept abstracted from relations of movement. The concept, therefore,

is founded not on the substances themselves but on their relations, whereas the moving substance itself is the basis of the mechanistic view.

(Jung, 1928, CW 8: para. 3)

Lacan (1977: 153) redefined the Freudian libido, not as substance, but as 'the effective presence, as such, of desire'. He too condemned Jung: 'Jungianism . . . is necessarily accompanied by a repudiation of the term *libido*, by the neutralization of this function by recourse to a notion of psychical energy, a much more generalized notion of interest' (ibid.: 153). Lacan's translator, Sheridan, points out that whereas the English word 'desire' is limited to isolated acts of wishing, the French *désir* 'has the stronger implication of a continuous force', and this meaning enters Lacan's theory as 'a perceptual effect of symbolic articulation' (ibid.: 278). The difference between that and the 'much more generalized notion of interest' of which Lacan accuses Jung is subtle indeed. One way to understand the 'effective presence of desire' would cast it as a causal factor, an intentional mode that we must switch into before we desire this or that, like contracting the illness before displaying the symptoms. Another way to understand it renders talk of causality nonsensical. We do not enter a 'looking' mode before looking at this or that object. When Jung introduced libido as a concept that 'expands into a conception of intentionality in general', his use of the word *intentionality* does not refer to motivation (intention) but to attunement to being, using the word as in phenomenology. Intentionality is to the intending subject as sight is to looking. Jung's claim that libido is present in all our psychological processes 'without ever being itself a specific instinct' is best read as placing the concept in an altogether different category from concepts such as instincts, intentions and desires. According to Jung, libido belongs with quantitative concepts such as energy: 'the concept of libido in psychology has functionally the same significance as the concept of energy in physics' (1952, CW 5: para. 189).

Jung quotes Schopenhauer by way of indicating his own line of thought (1952, CW 5: para. 197). In the section quoted by Jung, Schopenhauer (1922[1844]) distinguished Will-in-itself from its phenomenal appearances, reasoning that the abstract concept of *force* is derived from sense perception. Force is an Idea, an objectification. He contrasted the derived idea of force with the concept of Will which 'has its source *not* in the phenomenal . . . but comes from within, and proceeds from the most immediate consciousness of each of us' – adding, 'for here the subject and object of knowledge are one' (ibid.: 145). Schopenhauer discussed Will as a property of the natural universe, not of human minds, regarding it as the dynamic underlying the lawful organization of all types of phenomena. It is a concept akin to the idea of cosmic energy (and Schopenhauer acknowledges the significance of Indian doctrines for his metaphysics). Some scholars view Schopenhauer's Will as a precursor of Freud's concepts of the unconscious and id (Young and Brook, 1994) and Foucault's concept of power (Mather, 2000). The family resemblance of all those concepts should not distract us from Jung's specific point. In citing Schopenhauer, he tried to amplify the meaning of psychic energy as a quantitative concept 'abstracted from relations of movement' which must not be confused with the qualitative concept of force. Almost everyone uses the words 'energy' and 'force' interchangeably, so semantics-wise Jung's argument was doomed. It was doubly confounded by the reference to 'will'. Schopenhauer's concept does not imply a freedom to control one's behaviour (i.e. willpower) – but some Jungians mistakenly say that Jung insisted on 'freedom of will' (cited in Jones, 2002b). He doesn't; at least, not in his postulation of psychic energy. If the semantically loaded terminology of libido, energy and will is replaced with a neutral 'X', Jung's argument goes something like this:

–   There is X, which is not derived from sense perception and is also not desire (which is a definite thing). It is the *way* in which phenomena (including one's desires) become organized in our immediate experience.
–   Therefore, we cannot know X by looking at the external world. We intuit it from within our being.
–   In order to be accessible to the intellect, there must be some concrete representations of X. Therefore, the 'feel' of it is projected outward and objectified in concrete fantasy images (the sun god, fire, etc.).

However, Jung did not use an empty term like X. The 'pure' concept towards which he strives more clearly in the 1928 essay is confounded by a metaphor enabled by modern science, and ends up sounding like 'science mythology'.

Jung's case for revising the libido concept in the 1912 monograph, introduced there by querying the applicability of Freud's sexual-energy notion to certain clinical phenomena, leads into lengthy dense lucubration about myths of the sun god, fire and related etymologies (slightly 'stream-lined' in the 1952 revision). Jung grounds all those in bodily sensations of rhythm. In cognitive linguistics, Lakoff and Johnson (1980) similarly link idiomatic language to unconscious metaphors based in basic bodily experiences (on their thesis and Freudian libidinal theory, see Melnick, 1997). However, Jung only describes where certain imagery comes from so as to answer *why* such symbols – which are far more complex than language idioms – come into being. In contrast with Freud, no 'special chemistry' is involved in Jung's redefinition of the libido. Rather than proposing a 'psychical instinctual force in general', as Freud accused him of doing, Jung was at pains to locate symbol formation *in opposition* to the instinctual. The 'will to suppress or repress the natural instincts . . . derives from a spiritual source; in other words, the determining factor is the numinous primordial images' (1952, CW 5: para. 223). Bearing in mind that 'whether energy is God or God is energy' concerned him very little, his reference to a spiritual source could be translated in terms of psychological processes. Understood thus, Jung implies that the human organism transcends its instinctual existence by means of symbolic representations of its own typical situations ('primordial images', archetypes), productions that have intense psychological value (are 'numinous'). Whereas instincts are *'typical modes of action'*, archetypes are *'typical modes of apprehension'* (1948b, CW 8: paras. 273, 280; original emphasis). He suggests that the archetype 'might suitably be described as the instinct's perception of itself' (ibid.: para. 277). The anthropomorphism of instincts perceiving themselves is not particularly helpful towards building up a theory, but as a rhetorical device it amplifies the Heraclitean duality that Jung was striving to establish. 'The same psychic system which, on the one side, is based on the concupiscence of the instincts, rests on the other side on an opposing will which is at least as strong as the biological urge' (1952, CW 5: para. 222). He would make the same general point time and again, arriving at it from many different directions. His demonstration of the mutual exclusiveness of Freud's and Adler's theories of neurosis, mentioned in Chapter 1, is accompanied by the contention that both are 'destructive and reductive':

> For the human psyche . . . cannot be explained *solely* by reduction. Eros is certainly always and everywhere present, the urge to power certainly pervades the heights and depths of the psyche, but the psyche is not *just* the one or the other, nor . . . both together. It is *also* what it has made and will make out of them.
>
> (Jung, 1943, CW 7: para. 67)

Towards listing the characteristics of Jung's theorizing, the point to note is Jung's commitment to what James (1890: I, 218) specified as the psychologist's attitude of 'thoroughgoing dualism' which 'supposes two elements, mind knowing and thing known, and treats them as irreducible'.

Jung's concept of psychic energy enters the duality of the psyche making something out of the instincts (so to speak) as the dynamic of our oscillation between those two dimensions of human existence. The next section will identify a parallel with a view of Eros that Plato attributes to Heraclitus. But Jung stayed closer to home – namely, Freud – and his effort to specify the dynamics of such oscillation end up sounding like the mechanics of libidinal flows. Beginning the 1928 essay with an argument against placing 'libido' in causal-mechanistic explanations, Jung ends up telling us that a symbol is a 'psychological mechanism that transforms energy' (Jung, 1928, CW 8: para. 88). He proposes that the capacity to form symbols evolved as means for channelling surplus energy. Libidinal channelling takes the form of regression or progression. In progression,

> [The] damming up of libido is analogous to a specific obstruction in the
> direction of the flow, such as a dike, which transforms the kinetic
> energy of the flow into the potential energy of the reservoir. Thus
> dammed back, the water is forced into another channel.
>
> (Ibid.: para. 72)

Such metaphor-speak obscures Jung's basic and valid premise that the
appearance of symbolic productions in someone's activities coincides with
transformations in the personal situation. Why not drop all mentions of
libido or energy? One reason might be that Jung was in the grip of a
powerful metaphor, far more enduring and universal than the energy
metaphor borrowed from physics.

The stream of desire

In the *Dharmapada* we read: 'When the thirty-six streams of desire that run
towards pleasure are strong, their powerful waves carry away that man';
and hear the advice, 'Go beyond the stream . . . go with all your soul: leave
desires behind' (Mascaró, 1973: §§339, 383). In Freud, for whom libido
(Latin for *desire*) is sexual energy, we read about libidinal flow; e.g. 'a
collateral filling of subsidiary channels when the main stream has been
blocked by "repression"' (1953: 232). But here the stream analogy merges
into a modern mechanistic metaphor of energy as a motivating force. The
stream becomes steam power. In Jung, we read:

> Just as the libido may be compared to a steady stream pouring its
> waters into the world of reality, so a resistance [to sexual desire] . . .
> resembles, not a rock that juts up from the river-bed and causes the
> stream to flow around it, but a flowing back towards the source. Part of
> the psyche really wants the external object, but another part of it strives
> back to the subjective world, where the airy and lightly built palaces of
> fantasy beckon.
>
> (1952, CW 5: para. 253)

Here the 'stream' undergoes a further subtle mutation, losing the 'desire'
and instead becoming a vortex of fantasy production within which the
existential duality of desire and resistance becomes expressed and thus
knowable.

Unlike the *Dharmapada*, which teaches how one ought to live, both Freud
and Jung inform us about why we live as we do: this is human nature (they
say). Whereas Freud describes processes of motivation, Jung describes
processes of selective attention. They do so by means of an identical analogy
that, knowingly or not, was inherited from Plato. In 1912, Jung referred to

the stream analogy in Freud's *Three Essays*. Jung (ibid.: para. 190) noted that, according to Freud, the libido is 'divisible, can be dammed up, overflows into collaterals, and so on'; and through such 'libidinal affluxes' what is originally sexual can be communicated to non-sexual functions. As Freud put it, 'the preponderance of perverse tendencies in psychoneurotics' is explainable 'as a collateral filling of subsidiary channels when the main stream has been blocked by "repression"' (1953: 232). In *Republic*, Plato (1993: 485d) suggested that 'anyone whose predilection tends strongly in a single direction has correspondingly less desire for other things, like a stream whose flow has been diverted into another channel'. He gives thirst as an example of a desire that distracts a person from other pursuits, e.g. the desire for knowledge and truth. Plato delineates three kinds of desire (desires that satisfy the instincts, preserve a sense of self, and seek knowledge and truth), concluding that *desiring* is separate from the nature of the particular desire (439e). Jung makes a similar argument when he seeks to disengage libido from its qualitative coloration.

Neither Freud nor Jung mentioned Plato's stream analogy in relation to the libido (to my knowledge). Instead, in the 1920 Preface to the fourth edition of the *Three Essays* Freud mentions in passing 'how closely the enlarged sexuality of psycho-analysis coincides with the Eros of the divine Plato', citing a 1915 article that compares the Freudian theory with Plato's Eros (1953: 134). Ever since (it seems), scholars reading Plato were inclined to fuse Eros with Plato's stream. Yet it is Freud, not Plato, who upheld Eros (equated by him with sexual excitation) as universally the strongest motivating force – a claim that seemed justified in view of evolution, human biology and energy, as understood in Freud's time, and which was not possible in Plato's time. Moline (1981: 77–8) suggested that Plato's 'famous hydraulic simile' could clarify the meaning of that passage:

> The parts of the psyche are like channels or tubes into which the flow of a single stream is divided. The total flowage is constant, so that what goes into one tube or channel is lost to the others . . . Both the *Republic* and the *Symposium* suggest that this single source is *eros*, a primordial energy source powering not simply the stereotypically erotic activities, but all human activities whatsoever.

A similar reading was provided by Teloh (1976), who took the stream analogy in the *Republic* as pivotal for understanding Plato's conception of the soul as psychic energy. The suggested link must be very subtle indeed or lost in the translations of *Republic* and *Symposium* that I consulted. Commenting on Teloh's paper, Osborne (1976) contends that his interpretation is not borne out by Plato's argument in the same context; and, furthermore, Plato provided numerous analogies for the soul, and there is no good reason to regard the stream as more important than any other analogy.

In *Theaetetus*, Plato-as-Socrates elaborates in quick succession two very different analogies, of which he makes greater use than he does of the stream in *Republic*. First, the soul is depicted as containing a block of wax upon which sense-impressions are made. Second, it is likened to an aviary for of all sorts of birds – 'some in flocks apart from the rest, some in small groups, and some solitary, flying in any direction' – standing for 'pieces of knowledge' (*Theaetetus*, Plato, 1992: 197e). These and other analogies serve Plato's Socrates as heuristics or pedagogical devices, drawing attention to specific mental functions that he wants to emphasize in the context of various ongoing dialogues. None is asserted by Plato as the correct model of the mind or soul. Like that aviary, the Socratic dialogues are replete with ideas and concepts flying about separately, some in flocks and some solitary, and we get hold of them according to our skill and position. Plato does not link the stream analogy in *Republic* to Eros (his specific example for a desire is thirst, as mentioned). It is Freud who indirectly made it possible to see Plato's stream analogy and his discussion of Eros elsewhere like birds of a feather. It seems anachronistic to attribute to Plato an understanding of the Greek love-god as psychic energy. The Ancients did not have the modern mechanistic concept of energy that underpins Freudian thinking, and did not think in terms of body–mind dualism but in terms of animate and inanimate entities (as also noted by Teloh, 1976).

What exactly is Plato's Eros? Bemoaning philosophers' understatement of sexual love, Schopenhauer noted that Plato did address it – 'Yet what he says on the subject is confined to the sphere of myths, fables, and jokes, and also for the most part concerns only the Greek love of youths' (1909[1844]: 338). Plato's *Symposium*, his most celebrated treatment of the topic, comprises six speeches about Love (i.e. Eros) and a seventh, which is about Socrates, made at a drinking party that allegedly took place many years earlier. The debate is related to Plato by someone who heard it from a guest who didn't partake in the debate. Through this literary device Plato places himself at a considerable distance from any of the opinions being conveyed. None of those is a forerunner of the Freudian view. Lust seems to matter only to the inebriated Alcibiades, who gatecrashes the party and recalls his attempt to seduce Socrates (and whose portrayal might carry a moral-political message that 'explains' the historical fate of the real Alcibiades later on: Mara, 2003). The more dignified speakers are at pains to disengage Eros from base sexual instinct. Earthly Love 'governs the passions of the vulgar' who are 'attracted by women as by boys' and whose 'desires are of the body rather than of the soul,' says Pausanias (*Symposium*, Plato, 1961: 181b). In contrast, the attributes of the heavenly Love 'have nothing of the female, but are altogether male' (ibid.). Aristophanes invokes the myth of how Zeus cut the original humans in half. Therefore 'the happiness of the whole human race . . . is to be found in the consummation of our love, and in the healing of our dissevered nature by finding each his proper mate'

(193c). In the *Three Essays*, Freud indeed mentions this myth (without mentioning Plato) as a 'poetic fable' that beautifully reflects the 'popular view of the sexual instinct', noting that it therefore 'comes as a great surprise' to learn of homosexual attraction (1953: 136). It might have come as a surprise to Freud to learn that, according to Aristophanes, there were three original sexes – male, female and hermaphrodites – who were cut in half, and that's why some men are attracted to men, and some women are attracted to women.

Socrates, speaking last (but for Alcibiades, who is yet to arrive), imparts the truth about Eros that he had learned from a priestess, Diotima, who was probably fictitious. If Plato's own view is conveyed through Socrates, it is intriguing that he should disown it by attributing it to a woman, the 'other' of the Athenian intellectual. Diotima's doctrine unfolds gradually through her dialogue with Socrates, reported verbatim in *Symposium*. Throughout, it is love of beauty and good that is being discussed. Eros is the passionate 'longing for happiness and for the good . . . in the various fields of business, athletics, philosophy and so on', she tells Socrates (Plato, 1961: 205d). Yet, it is a longing, 'not for the beautiful itself, but for the conception and generation that the beautiful effects' (206e). She reminds Socrates of 'the extraordinary effect that the breeding instinct has upon both animals and birds' (207b). Dismissing the longing-for-the-other-half myth, which applies only to humans, Diotima points to how obsessed animals are with the desire first to mate, then to rear their young and protect them. Eros is linked with procreation for this is 'the one deathless and eternal element in our mortality' (ibid.). For the same reason, men seek fame in great deeds that would ensure that their name survives their own death. But the highest form of Love possible for humans is that of abstract universal beauty. If a 'man's life is ever worth the living,' she says, 'it is when he has attained this vision of the very soul of beauty. And once you have seen it, you will never be seduced again by the charm of gold, of dress, of comely boys'; and so on (211d). The point made by Diotima-Socrates-Plato differs from Freud's in important ways. Whereas in Freudian mechanics, the 'special chemistry' of sexual excitation kicks the psyche into motion, in Plato's teleology, the thrust of life works through manifestations ranging from the most basic breeding instinct to the most refined *participation mystique* in the divine.

How would Jung fare in the *Symposium*? Socrates' speech is its philosophical highpoint, but the view of an earlier speaker would be more in keeping with Jung's outlook on the nature and structure of the psyche. Eryximachus, a medical doctor, points to the 'jarring elements of the body' in sickness and health (186d) so as to identify Love as a regulating principle. Quoting Heraclitus' pronouncement that 'The one in conflict with itself is held together, like the harmony of the bow and of the lyre' (187a), he contends that there is a kind of conflict that is not discord in need of resolution, but a dualism necessary for harmony and unity. Eryximachus gives examples such as rhythm, in music, which is produced by 'resolving the difference between fast and slow' (187c), and seasonal cold and hot, wet and dry, which in their proper balance bring health and plenty for humans, animals and plants. Via Eryximachus – whose Heraclitean 'voice' is marginalized in the *Symposium* – Plato presents a pre-Socratic account evocative of the yin–yang duality in ancient Chinese philosophy and Buddhist doctrines of change and soul. As mentioned in the previous chapter, Jung attributed to Heraclitus the discovery of the regulative function of opposites or *enantiodromia* (1921, CW 6). Pietikäinen (1999: 237) notes that Jung cites Ernst Cassirer's idea of 'attunement turning back on itself' when defining his own use of *enantiodromia* in *Gessammelle Werke* (the reference to Cassirer was removed in the English translation of Volume 6). Cassirer pointed out a tension between philosophies of becoming and of being in Ancient Greece: in contrast with Heraclitus' 'thesis of the "flux of things"', the Platonic Idea is 'purely present . . . always is and never becomes' (1955[1925]: 133). Heraclitus 'spoke in unforgettable images of the "stream of life" – that stream which irresistibly carries all Being along with it and in which no man can step twice' – yet his attention, according to Cassirer, is not on 'this mere fact of flowing and passing but is directed toward the eternal measures which he apprehends in it . . . the truly one and immutable logos of the world' (ibid.: 133). Citing Heraclitus' maxim that a hidden harmony is better than visible harmony, Cassirer concludes that

> On this . . . sure and necessary rhythm which is maintained in all change, rests the certainty 'of a hidden harmony that is better than the visible harmony.' It is only in order to assure himself of this hidden harmony that Heraclitus turns back again and again to the contemplation of change.
>
> (Ibid.: 134)

Similarly, Jung speaks of psychic energy as 'fluid' relations of movement; but it is the certainty of a hidden harmony, the immutable logos of the psyche, that he ultimately seeks.

We cannot step into the same stream twice, Heraclitus famously said. Stepping into Plato's stream analogy after Freud, some scholars find Eros there and, furthermore, redefine Plato's Eros as a primordial energy source powering human activities. How should we step into the stream after Jung? His reformulation of the libido does not write off the stream analogy, but alters its application. If, with Plato and Freud, we see the stream as if standing on its bank, with Jung and Heraclitus we ought to imagine ourselves like a grain of sand carried by its torrent, experiencing it from within. Jung's 1928 essay labours more clearly towards a concept of dynamism as an abstract property of the psyche in the sense that flow is a property of a stream. If with Freud we see the libido as channelled, blocked, diverted or dispersed unequally across various channels, with Jung we would ask what it 'feels like' to be caught in the turbulence.

Postmodern closures

Two powerful 'technological' metaphors – energy and information – have shaped psychologists' quest to comprehend the human power of comprehension. Mentions of mental energy were as common in textbooks published during the first half of the last century as references to information processing are in textbooks published in the second half. The idea of the psyche as activated by energy of sorts was perhaps intuitively appealing to a generation that saw the first motor cars and use of electricity. The idea of the mind as an information-processing machine might seem intuitively correct to a generation that saw the computer revolution. The informational bias is reproduced in postmodern psychology, which basically relocates the 'processing' to actual discourse and discursive practices.

Certain connotations of the energy metaphor did not survive the transition to the discourses of information, but remain familiar to us in common speech. Energy is often spoken of as vigour or vitality, of being 'full of life', the opposite of fatigue or lethargy. This meaning is implicit in William James' (1907) lecture, 'The energies of men', which he presented to the American Philosophical Association. At least in English, it dates to the nineteenth century, according to the Oxford English Dictionary Online (retrieved March 2006). It is consistent with the oldest usage of the word identified by the *OED*, dated to the sixteenth century: energy as force or vigour of expression in speech or writing. This meaning is attributed to Late Latin and is considered as derived from Aristotle's use of the Greek word *energia* for 'the species of metaphor which calls up a mental picture of something "acting" or moving' (*OED*). In nineteenth-century philosophies of nature, an idea of vitality and life was expanded into vitalism, associated with the postulation of a life force that animates organisms. That association fuels criticisms of Bergson's idea of *élan vital*; and it is the vitalism of which Jung is sometimes accused. Neither Jung nor Bergson deserves the criticism. Bergson's (1911) *élan vital* could be understood as a property of nature that is expressed in all living things (by definition), as opposed to something that causes things to come to life. In a similar way, to speak colloquially of someone as being 'full of energy' describes a personality trait or state, not what brought it about. Although Jung's 'psychic energy' should likewise be viewed as the identification of an intrinsic property of the psyche, it is not vitality. It is something else.

Jung's statement about psychic energy and misconceptions about what he was saying cut a different channel of knowledge formation from the above. In the early twentieth century, speculations about mental or 'psychical' energy were closely linked to discussions of energy in nineteenth-century physics and (consequently) physiology, especially in the German intellectual world. The *OED* defines the meaning of energy in physics as the 'power of "doing work" possessed at any instant by a body or system of bodies'. The dictionary notes that it was first used to denote the power of doing work possessed by a moving body by virtue of its motion, now called actual (kinetic, motive) energy, later extended to include potential (static, latent) energy, and other energies, such as mechanical, molecular, chemical, electrical, etc. The notion of multiple kinds of energy made it possible to speak also of mental energies and their varieties (sexual, aggressive, etc.). There were variations on the theme, not just from psychologists. To cite but one, Wilhelm Ostwald – who was awarded the Nobel Prize in 1909 for his work in chemistry and was centrally associated with the energetics movement – suggested a formula for happiness, which expresses mathematically his idea that happiness is determined entirely by quantities of energy (Hakfoort, 1992). When 'energy' travelled to the psychoanalytical discourse, however, it lost the mathematical grounding of theorizing about it as in physics. Here, talk of energy became entirely qualitative. In a similar way, to speak of electric *current* reinforces the picture of something that flows in cables, like water in pipes, though we know better with a little physics. No description analogous to the scientific explanation of what an electric current really is was forthcoming in psychology. This was the entrenched thinking that Jung spiritedly confronted. He contested the hypostasized concept of energy, 'an example of the superstitious overvaluation of facts' (1921, CW 6: para. 699). But he too continued to speak of libidinal flows and blockages as a legitimate scientific explanation.

The energy metaphor entered academic psychology differently from how it entered Jung's immediate milieu. In his 'Energies of men' talk, James commented on how little use European psychiatrists made of the 'machinery' usually relied on by psychologists, noting their 'own reliance on conceptions which in the laboratories and in scientific publications we never hear of at all' (1907: 321). Early on, some psychologists (e.g. Wundt) sought continuities with physiology. A connection with physiological arousal might seem obvious (see Vernon, 1969). However, by the 1930s, 'mental energy' was assimilated into theorizing about human motivation as a distinctly psychological concept. In *The Energies of Men*, first published in 1932, William McDougall regarded the concept as indispensable: 'In view of the purposive nature of human activity . . . [we] must postulate some energy which conforms to laws not wholly identical with the laws of energy stated by the physical sciences. We may provisionally speak of it as mental energy' (1950: 10). He immediately moves from the provisional to the scientific-sounding by renaming it *psycho-physical energy* and proceeding to coin '*hormic energy* . . . meaning an urge or impulse towards a goal; it thus points to the distinctive rôle of the postulated energy, marks it as the energy peculiar to purposive activities' (ibid.: 10; original emphasis). To speak of *psychic* energy, he opined, is to 'make far-reaching assumptions about psychic realities independent of the physical realm', assumptions that are 'best avoided as highly controversial' (ibid.: 10, n. 1). McDougall intended his concept of hormic energy to forge connections between processes of the body and processes of the mind within a unified science of psychology (which had no room for psychoanalytical doctrines, in his view). In effect, concepts such as hormic energy compound the body–mind problem, and were treated by more cautious writers as a metaphor at best. Another textbook first published in the 1930s described 'a human being's behaviour as if it were activated by a fund of energy which, like physical energy, can be directed into one channel or another' – warning, 'It is an analogy that must not be pressed too far' (Thouless, 1951: 30). The analogy was still pressed in the 1950s, but the tide was turning.

The energy metaphor lost its *energeia*, its power to move us, in the age of information. A closure on 'energy' in mainstream psychology came about in several ways. Rhetorical closure was put into motion by the behaviourists who ridiculed mental energy as unscientific. A closure by redefinition of the problem came about with the discovery of the computer metaphor. Meanwhile, psychoanalytical discourses underwent various reinterpretations that effectively put a closure on the energy metaphor. The borrowing of terminology from physics was still 'hot' enough to problematize in the 1960s (see Shope, 1971), but soon new interpretations of Freud opened up possibilities for placing the 'effective presence of desire' in language and the dynamics of discourse. 'Energy' became replaced by 'power'. In the language game of postmodernism, we see that we exist by virtue of our positioning within power relations effected within discursive practices:

> The customary model . . . goes as follows: power imposes itself on us, and, weakened by its force, we come to internalize or accept its terms. What such an account fails to note, however, is that 'we' who accept such terms are fundamentally dependent on those terms for 'our' existence.
>
> (Butler, 1997: 2)

The paradigm shift to discourse poses a dilemma of postmodern psychology. To paraphrase Shotter (earlier quotations), the ways in which our bodily reactions relate us to our surroundings remain rationally invisible. That rationally invisible Unknown continues to press itself into the known – and the *flow* metaphor re-surges with new vigour. We find our selves in our embodied embedding in the whole flow of temporally irreversible activity. We live 'a biography reflexively organized in terms of flows of social and psychological information about possible ways of life' (Giddens, 1991: 14). We realize that people 'produce a flow of action . . . forever producing and reproducing their own minds and the societies in which they live' (Harré, 1998: 15). If we are swept along by this vision of flow, we might be persuaded that individualistic psychologies such as Jung's are fallacious, a legacy of Descartes and the derided atomistic worldview:

> The urge to base psychology on something that is occurrent, observable in its fullness here and now, and that is also persistent, constant in its nature through space and time, has to be resisted. These demands are incompatible. What is occurrent is ephemeral.
>
> (Ibid.: 15)

But if we are swept along by the rhetoric of rediscovering human conscious-ness in discourse, we are likely to miss the 'point' of Jung's psychology of the unconscious.

Silently, Jung and postmodern psychology mirror each other back to back, facing away from each other, each reflecting something that is understated or dismissed in the discourse of the other. They reflect oppo-sites of post-Enlightenment psychology. This book attempted to articulate a space of questions that open up between those mirror reflections – a space opening up by virtue of their mutual opposition. It is a Moment in intellectual history at the close of the millennium. The 'new paradigm' described in this book already has its orthodoxy which is challenged from within by critical thinkers, and is eclipsed from without by the increasingly dominant discourse of neuroscience (but that's another story). Some things remain unchanged. A century since Jung began to ponder the emergence of meaning in human activities, the language games of psychology changed considerably, but we are still trying to link the Unknown to the Known, still trying to make our embodied existence visible in our sciences. One way or another, sooner or later, we return to ponder that Heraclitean hidden harmony or the sure and necessary rhythm which is maintained in all change (Cassirer), that silent and void 'way' that stands alone and does not change (Lao Tzu), the Unconscious (Jung).

References

Abarbanell, N. (1994) *Eva and Lilith* Ramat-Gan: Bar-Ilan University (In Hebrew)
Aristotle (1997) *Poetics* Mineola, NY: Dover (Original translation published in 1895)
Austin, S. (2005) *Women's Aggressive Fantasies* London: Routledge
Bachelard, G. (1994) *The Poetics of Space* Boston, MA: Beacon Press (Original work published 1958)
Bair, D. (2003) *Jung* Boston, MA: Little, Brown & Company
Bakhtin, M. M. (1981) *The Dialogic Imagination* Austin, TX: Texas University Press
—— (1984) *Problems of Dostoevsky's Poetics* Minneapolis, MN: University of Minneapolis Press (Original work published in 1963)
—— (1986) *Speech Genres and Other Late Essays* Austin, TX: University of Texas Press
—— (1993) *Toward a Philosophy of the Act* Austin, TX: University of Texas Press
Bamberg, M. (2006) 'Biographic-narrative research, *Quo Vadis?* A critical review of "Big Stories" from the perspective of "Small Stories"' In Kelly, N., Horrocks, C., Milnes, K., Roberts, B. and Robinson, D. (eds) *Narrative, Memory and Knowledge* Huddersfield: Huddersfield University Press
Barthes, R. (1993) *Mythologies* London: Vintage (Original work published in 1957)
Bayer, B. M. and Shotter, J. (eds) (1998) *Reconstructing the Psychological Subject* London: Sage
Beebe, J. (2002) 'An archetypal model of the self in dialogue' *Theory & Psychology* 12, 267–80
—— (2006) 'Psychological types' In Papadopoulos, R. K. (ed.) *The Handbook of Jungian Psychology* London: Routledge
Benjamin, W. (1999) *Illuminations* London: Pimlico (Originally published in 1936)
Bennet, E. A. (1983) *What Jung Really Said* New York: Schocken Books
—— (1985) *Meetings with Jung* Zurich: Daimon
Bergson, H. (1911) *Creative Evolution* Mineola, NY: Dover
Billig, M. (1999) *Freudian Repression* Cambridge: Cambridge University Press
Bleuler, E. (1913) 'Autistic thinking' *American Journal of Insanity* 69, 873–86
—— (1951) 'Autistic thinking' In Rapaport, D. (ed.) *Organization and Pathology of Thought* New York: Columbia University Press (Original work published in 1913)
Blofeld, J. (1962) *The Zen Teaching of Hui Hai* London: Rider & Company
Botella, L., Figueras, S., Herrero, O. and Pacheco, M. (1997) 'Qualitative analysis of

self-narratives: A constructivist approach to the storied nature of identity' workshop presented at The XIIth International Congress on Personal Construct Psychology, 9–12 July 1997, Seattle, Washington, USA

Bovensiepen, G. (2002) 'Symbolic attitude and reverie: problems of symbolization in children and adolescents' *Journal of Analytical Psychology* 47, 241–58

Brooke, R. (1991) *Jung and Phenomenology* London: Routledge

Brown, S. D., Pujol, J. and Curt, B. C. (1998) 'As one in a web? Discourse, materiality and the place of ethics' In Parker, I. (ed.) *Social Constructionism, Discourse and Realism* London: Sage

Bruner, J. S. (1986) *Actual Minds, Possible Worlds* Cambridge, MA: Harvard University Press

—— (1990) *Acts of Meaning* Cambridge, MA: Harvard University Press

—— (2004) *Making Stories* Cambridge, MA: Harvard University Press

Burkitt, I. (1999) 'Between the dark and the light: power and the material context of social relation' In Nightingale, D. J. and Cromby, J. (eds) *Social Constructionist Psychology* Milton Keynes: Open University Press

Butler, J. (1997) *The Psychic Life of Power* Stanford, CA: Stanford University Press

Cassirer, E. (1946) *Language and Myth* New York: Dover (Original work published 1925)

—— (1955) *The Philosophy of Symbolic Forms* (vol. 2) New Haven, CT: Yale University Press (Original work published in 1925)

Copjec, J. (1994) 'Sex and the euthanasia of reason' In Copjec, J. (ed.) *Supposing the Subject* London: Verso

Critchlow, N. (2003) 'The use of qualitative methods in the study of children's perceptions of teacher authority' Unpublished M.Sc. dissertation, School of Social Sciences, Cardiff University

Crossley, M. L. (2000) *Introducing Narrative Psychology* Milton Keynes: Open University Press

Danziger, K. (1983) 'Origins and basic principles of Wundt's *Völkerpsychologie*' *British Journal of Social Psychology* 22, 303–13

—— (1997) *Naming the Mind* London: Sage

Davies, B. and Harré, R. (1990) 'Positioning: the discursive production of selves' *Journal for the Theory of Social Behaviour* 20, 43–64

Dawson, T. (2004) *The Effective Protagonist in the Nineteenth-Century British Novel* Ashgate: Aldershot & Burlington

Deleuze, G. (1988) *Foucault* London: Athlone Press

Derrida, J. (1978) *Writing and Difference* London: Routledge (Original work published 1967)

Dodds, A. E., Lawrence, J. A. and Valsiner, J. (1997) 'The personal and the social: Mead's theory of the "Generalized Other"' *Theory & Psychology* 7, 483–503

Durkheim, E. and Mauss, M. (1963) *Primitive Classification* London: Cohen & West (Original work published 1903)

Edwards, D. and Potter, J. (1992) *Discursive Psychology* London: Sage

Erikson, E. H. (1968) *Identity* London: Faber & Faber

Feyerabend, P. (1993) *Against Method* (3rd edn) London: Verso

Flew, A. (1979) *A Dictionary of Philosophy* London: Pan

Forster, E. M. (1974) *Aspects of the Novel* London: Edward Arnold (Original work published in 1927)

Foucault, M. (1989) *The Archaeology of Knowledge* London: Routledge (Original work published in 1969)

—— (1991) *Discipline and Punish* London: Penguin (Original work published 1975)

Freeman, M. (1997) 'Why narrative? Hermeneutics, historical understanding, and the significance of stories' *Journal of Narrative and Life History* 7, 169–76

Freud, S. (1953) 'Three essays on the theory of sexuality' *The Standard Edition of the Complete Psychological Works* (vol. VII) London: Hogarth Press (Original work published in 1905)

—— (1974) 'Resistance and repression' *Introductory Lectures on Psychoanalysis* Harmondsworth: Penguin (Original work published in 1917)

—— (1976) *The Interpretation of Dreams* Harmondsworth: Penguin (Original work published 1900)

—— (1984) 'Formulations on the principles of mental functioning' *The Penguin Freud Library* (vol. 11) Harmondsworth: Penguin (Original work published in 1911)

Frye, N. (1957) *Anatomy of Criticism* Princeton, NJ: Princeton University Press

Gadamer, H.-G. (1976) *Philosophical Hermeneutics* Berkeley, CA: University of California Press

Gallagher, S. (2000) 'Philosophical conceptions of the self: implications for cognitive science' *Trends in Cognitive Sciences* 4, 14–21

Gergen, K. J. (1994) *Realities and Relationships* Cambridge, MA: Harvard University Press

—— (1997) 'The place of the psyche in a constructed world' *Theory & Psychology* 7, 723–46

Giddens, A. (1991) *Modernity and Self-Identity* Cambridge: Polity

Gras, V. W. (1981) 'Myth and the reconciliation of opposites: Jung and Lévi-Strauss' *Journal of the History of Ideas* 42, 471–88

Gullestad, M. (1996) *Everyday Life Philosophers* Oslo: Scandinavian University Press

Gunter, P. A. Y. (1982) Bergson and Jung *Journal of the History of Ideas* 43, 635–52

Hakfoort, C. (1992) 'Science defied: Wilhelm Ostwald's energeticist world-view and the history of scientism' *Annals of Science* 49, 525–44

Harding, E. (1963) *Psychic Energy* (2nd edn) Princeton, NJ: Princeton University Press

Harré, R. (1997) 'Forward to Aristotle: the case for a hybrid ontology' *Journal for the Theory of Social Behaviour* 27, 173–92

—— (1998) *The Singular Self* London: Sage

—— (2005) *Key Thinkers in Psychology* London: Sage

Harré, R. and van Langenhove, L. (1991) 'Varieties of positioning' *Journal for the Theory of Social Behaviour* 21, 393–408

—— (eds) (1999) *Positioning Theory* Oxford: Blackwell

Hauke, C. (2000) *Jung and the Postmodern* London: Routledge

Heidelberger, M. (2003) 'The mind–body problem in the origin of logical empiricism: Herbert Feigl and psychophysical parallelism' In Parrini, P. and Salmon, W. (eds) *Logical Empiricism: Historical and Contemporary Perspectives* Pittsburgh, PA: Pittsburgh University Press

Henriques, J., Hollway, W., Urwin, C., Venn, C. and Walkerdine, V. (1994) *Changing the Subject* London: Routledge (Original work published in 1984)

Hepburn, A. (1999) 'Derrida and psychology: deconstruction and its ab/uses in critical and discursive psychologies' *Theory & Psychology* 9, 639–66

Hermans, H. J. M. (1993) 'Moving opposites in the self: a Heraclitean approach' *Journal of Analytical Psychology* 38, 437–62

—— (1999) 'Self-narrative as meaning construction: the dynamics of self-investigation' *Journal of Clinical Psychology* 55, 1193–1211

—— (2000) 'The coherence of incoherent narratives' *Narrative Inquiry* 10, 223–7

—— (2001a) 'The dialogical self: toward a theory of personal and cultural positioning' *Culture & Psychology* 7, 243–81

—— (2001b) 'The construction of a personal position repertoire: method and practice' *Culture & Psychology* 7, 323–66

—— (2002) 'The dialogical self as a society of mind: introduction' *Theory & Psychology* 12, 147–60

Hermans, H. J. M. and Kempen, H. J. G. (1993) *The Dialogical Self* San Diego, CA: Academic Press

Hermans, H. J. M., Kempen, H. J. G. and van Loon, R. J. P. (1992) 'The dialogical self: beyond individualism and rationalism' *American Psychologist* 47, 23–33

Hevern, V. W. (2006) 'Narrative psychology: basics' *Narrative Psychology: Internet and Resource Guide* Available <www.narrativepsychology.com> (accessed 28 June 2006)

Hillman, J. (1975) *Re-Visioning Psychology* New York: Harper Perennial

—— (1983) *Healing Fiction* Woodstock, CT: Spring

Hogenson, G. B. (2006) 'What are symbols symbols of? Situated action, mythological bootstrapping and the emergence of the Self' *Journal of Analytical Psychology* 49, 67–82

Hollway, W. and Jefferson, T. (2000) *Doing Qualitative Research Differently* London: Sage

Holquist, M. (2002) *Dialogism* (2nd edn) London: Routledge

Homans, P. (1995) *Jung in Context* (2nd edn) Chicago, IL: The University of Chicago Press

James, W. (1890) *The Principles of Psychology* New York: Holt

—— (1902) *The Varieties of Religious Experience: A Study in Human Nature* London: Longmans, Green and Co

—— (1907) 'The energies of men' *Science* 25, 321–32

Jones, R. A. (1995) *The Child–School Interface* London: Cassell

—— (1997) 'The presence of self in the person: reflexive positioning and personal construct psychology' *Journal for the Theory of Social Behaviour* 27, 102–19

—— (1999) 'Direct perception and symbol forming in positioning' *Journal for the Theory of Social Behaviour* 29, 37–58

—— (2001) 'Psychological value and symbol formation' *Theory & Psychology* 11, 233–54

—— (2002a) 'The necessity of the unconscious' *Journal for the Theory of Social Behaviour* 32, 344–65

—— (2002b) 'Self and place in "The White Light" by Amalia Kahana-Carmon' *Textual Practice* 16, 93–110

—— (2002c) 'The relational premises of Jung's theory of psychological value and the embodied symbol' In Shohov, S. P. (ed.) *Trends in Cognitive Psychology* Hunnington, NY: Nova Science

—— (2003a) 'Between the analytical and the critical: implications for theorizing the self' *Journal of Analytical Psychology* 48, 355–70

—— (2003b) 'Mixed metaphors and narrative shifts: archetypes' *Theory & Psychology* 13, 651–72

—— (2003c) 'Jung's view on myth and post-modern psychology' *Journal of Analytical Psychology* 48, 619–28

—— (2003d) 'On innatism: a response to Hogenson' *Journal of Analytical Psychology* 48, 705–18

—— (2004) 'The science and meaning of the self' *Journal of Analytical Psychology* 49, 217–33

Jung, C. G. Unless otherwise stated, the following are from *The Collected Works of C. G. Jung* (CW) London: Routledge & Kegan Paul/Princeton, NJ: Princeton University Press:

—— (1907) 'The psychology of dementia praecox' (CW 3)

—— (1919) *Psychology of the Unconscious* London: Kegan Paul, Trench, Turner & Co. (Original work published in 1912)

—— (1921) *Psychological types* (CW 6)

—— (1922) 'On the relation of analytical psychology to poetry' (CW 15)

—— (1927) 'Mind and the earth' In Baynes, H. G. and Baynes, C. F. (eds) *Contributions to Analytical Psychology* London: Kegan Paul

—— (1928) 'On psychic energy' (CW 8)

—— (1931a) 'Basic postulates of analytical psychology' (CW 8)

—— (1931b) 'The structure of the psyche' (CW 8)

—— (1931) 'Mind and earth' (CW 10)

—— (1934) 'A review of the complex theory' (CW 8)

—— (1934) 'The practical use of dream-analysis' (CW 16)

—— (1935) 'The Tavistock lectures' (CW 18)

—— (1936) 'The concept of the collective unconscious' (CW 9I)

—— (1936) 'Wotan' (CW 10)

—— (1943) 'On the psychology of the unconscious' (CW 7)

—— (1944) 'Psychology and alchemy' (CW 12)

—— (1946) 'Analytical psychology and education' (CW 17)

—— (1948) 'The phenomenology of the spirit in fairytales' (CW 9I)

—— (1948a) 'The psychological foundations of belief in spirits' (CW 8)

—— (1948b) 'Instinct and the unconscious' (CW 8)

—— (1948c) 'On the nature of dreams' (CW 8)

—— (1950) 'Psychology and literature' (CW 15)

—— (1951) 'Aion' (CW 9II)

—— (1951) 'Synchronicity: an acausal connecting principle' (CW 8)

—— (1951) 'The psychological aspects of the Kore' (CW 9I)

—— (1952) 'Symbols of transformation' (CW 5)

—— (1954) 'On the nature of the psyche' (CW 8)

—— (1954) 'Psychological aspects of the mother archetype' (CW 9I)

—— (1957) 'Forward to Michael Fordham: new developments in analytical psychology' (CW 18)

—— (1958) 'The transcendent function' (CW 8)

—— (1961) 'Symbols and the interpretation of dreams' (CW 18)

—— (1963) *Memories, Dreams, Reflections* London: Collins and Routledge & Kegan Paul

—— (1964) 'Approaches to the unconscious' In Jung, C. G. and von Franz, M.-L. (eds) *Man and His Symbols* London: Picador

—— (1989) *Analytical Psychology: Notes of the Seminar Given in 1925* Princeton, NJ: Princeton University Press (Original work published 1926)

Kant, I. (1933) *Critique of Pure Reason* London: Macmillan (Original work published in 1781)

Kelly, G. A. (1963) *A Theory of Personality* New York: Norton

Kelly, M. P. and Dickinson, H. (1997) 'The narrative self in autobiographical accounts of illness' *Sociological Review* 45, 254–78

Kerslake, C. (2004) 'Rebirth through incest: on Deleuze's early Jungianism' *Angelaki* 9, 135–56

Kirsch, T. (2000) *The Jungians* London: Routledge

Köhler, W. (1930) *Gestalt Psychology* London: Bell and Sons

Kristeva, J. (1980) *Desire in Language* Oxford: Blackwell

Kusch, M. (1995) *Psychologism* London: Routledge

Kvale, S. (ed.) (1992) *Psychology and Postmodernism* London: Sage

Lacan, J. (1977) *The Four Fundamental Concepts of Psychoanalysis* Harmondsworth: Penguin

Lakoff, G. and Johnson, M. (1980) *Metaphors We Live By* Chicago, IL: University of Chicago Press

Lao Tzu (1963) *Tao Te Ching* Harmondsworth: Penguin

Lewin, K. (1935) *A Dynamic Theory of Personality* New York: McGraw-Hill

Lincoln, B. (1999) *Theorizing Myth* Chicago, IL: University of Chicago Press

Lu K'uan Yü (1961) *Ch'an and Zen Teaching* London: Rider & Company

Lyotard, J.-F. (1984) *The Postmodern Condition* Manchester: Manchester University Press (Original work published in 1979)

McAdams, D. P. (1985) *Power, Intimacy and the Life Story* Homewood, IL: The Dorsey Press

—— (1993) *The Stories We Live By* New York: Guilford Press

—— (1998) 'Ego, trait, identity' In Westenberg, P. M., Blasi, A. and Cohn, L. D. (eds) *Personality Development* Mahwah, NJ: Erlbaum

—— (1999) 'Personal narratives and the life story' In Pervin, L. A. and John, O. P. (eds) *Handbook of Personality* (2nd edn) New York: Guilford Press

—— (2000) 'The narrative study of lives: principles, themes, and controversies' Paper presented at the First International Conference on the Dialogical Self, Nijmegen, The Netherlands, 23–26 June 2000

—— (2001) 'The psychology of life stories' *Review of General Psychology* 5, 100–22

McAdams, D. P., Reynolds, J., Lewis, M., Patten, A. H. and Bowman, P. J. (2001) 'When bad things turn good and good things turn bad: sequences of redemption and contamination in life narrative and their relation to psychosocial adaptation in midlife adults and in students' *Personality & Social Psychology Bulletin* 27, 474–85

McDougall, W. (1950) *The Energies of Men* (8th edn) London: Methuen

McDowell, M. J. (2001) 'Principle of organization: a dynamic-system view of the archetype-as-such' *Journal of Analytical Psychology* 46, 637–54

MacIntyre, A. (1984) *After Virtue* (2nd edn) Paris: University of Notre Dame Press

McLeod, J. (1997) *Narrative and Psychotherapy* London: Sage

Mair, M. (1988) 'Psychology as storytelling' *International Journal of Personal Construct Psychology* 1, 125–37

Malinowski, B. (1971) *Myth in Primitive Psychology* Westport, CT: Negro Universities Press (Originally published in 1926)

Mara, G. M. (2003) 'Democratic self-criticism and the other in classical political theory' *The Journal of Politics* 65, 739–58

Marková, I. and Foppa, K. (eds) (1990) *The Dynamics of Dialogue* New York: Harvester Wheatsheaf

Mascaró, J. (1973) *Dharmapada* Harmondsworth: Penguin

Mather, R. (2000) 'The foundations of critical psychology' *History of the Human Sciences* 13, 85–100

Mead, G. H. (1934) *Mind, Self, and Society* Chicago, IL: University of Chicago Press

—— (1938) *The Philosophy of the Act* Chicago, IL: University of Chicago Press

Melnick, B. A. (1997) 'Metaphor and the theory of libidinal development' *International Journal of Psychoanalysis* 78, 997–1015

Moline, J. (1981) *Plato's Theory of Understanding* Madison, WI: University of Wisconsin Press

Nightingale, D. J. and Cromby, J. (eds) (1999) *Social Constructionist Psychology* Milton Keynes: Open University Press

O'Connor, K. P. and Hallam, R. S. (2000) 'Sorcery of the self: the magic of you' *Theory & Psychology* 10, 238–64

Olney, J. (1972) *Metaphors of Self* Princeton, NJ: Princeton University Press

—— (1980) 'Autobiography and the cultural movement: a thematic, historical and bibliographical introduction' In Olney, J. (ed.) *Autobiography Essays* Princeton, NJ: Princeton University Press

Osborne, M. L. (1976) 'On the image of the soul as a stream in Plato's *Republic*' *The Southern Journal of Philosophy* XIV (3), 359–63

Papadopoulos, R. K. (1984) 'Jung and the concept of the Other' In Papadopoulos, R. K. and Saayman, G. S. (eds) *Jung in Modern Perspective* Middlesex: Wildwood House

—— (ed.) (2006) *The Handbook of Jungian Psychology* London: Routledge

Parker, I. (1989) *The Crisis in Modern Social Psychology, and How to End It* London: Routledge

—— (1999) 'Introduction: varieties of discourse and analysis' In Parker, I. (ed.) *Critical Textwork* Milton Keynes: Open University Press

—— (2005) 'Lacanian discourse analysis in psychology: seven theoretical elements' *Theory and Psychology* 15, 163–82

Piaget, J. (1962) *Play, Dreams and Imitation in Childhood* London: Routledge & Kegan Paul

Pietikäinen, P. (1999) *C. G. Jung and the Psychology of Symbolic Forms* Helsinki: Academia Scientiarum Fennica

Plato (1961) 'Symposium' In Hamilton, E. and Cairns, H. (eds) *The Complete Dialogues of Plato* Princeton, NJ: Princeton University Press

—— (1992) *Theaetetus* Indianapolis, IN: Hackett

—— (1993) *Republic* Oxford: Oxford University Press

Polkinghorne, D. E. (1989) *Narrative Knowing and the Human Sciences* Albany, NY: State University of New York Press

—— (1992) 'Postmodern epistemology of practice' In Kvale, S. (ed.) *Psychology and Postmodernism* London: Sage

—— (1995) 'Narrative configuration in qualitative analysis' In Hatch, J. A. and Wisniewski, R. (eds) *Life History and Narrative* London: Falmer Press

Popper, K. R. (1958) *The Logic of Scientific Discovery* London: Hutchinson

Pratt, A. (1981) *Archetypal Patterns in Women's Fiction* Brighton: Harvester Press

Rapaport, D. (ed.) (1951) *Organization and Pathology of Thought* New York: Columbia University Press

Ricoeur, P. (1984) *Time and Narrative* (vol. 1) Trans. McLaughlin, K. and Pellauer, D. Chicago, IL: University of Chicago Press

Rieff, P. (1959) *Freud* London: Victor Gollancz

Riessman, C. K. (1993) *Narrative Analysis* Newbury Park, CA: Sage

Rorty, R. (1980) *Philosophy and the Mirror of Nature* Oxford: Blackwell

—— (1989) *Contingency, Irony, and Solidarity* Cambridge: Cambridge University Press

Rose, N. (1985) *The Psychological Complex* London: Routledge & Kegan Paul

Rowland, S. (2005) *Jung as Writer* London: Routledge

Ryan, B. A. (1999) 'Does postmodernism mean the end of science in the behavioral sciences, and does it matter anyway?' *Theory & Psychology* 9, 483–502

Rychlak, J. F. (1984) 'Jung as dialectician and teleologist' In Papadopoulos, R. K. and Saayman, G. S. (eds) *Jung in Modern Perspective* Middlesex: Wildwood House

Sampson, E. E. (1985) 'The decentralization of identity: toward a revised concept of personal and social order' *American Psychologist* 40, 1203–11

Samuels, A. (1985) *Jung and the Post-Jungians* London: Routledge & Kegan Paul

Sarbin, T. R. (1986) 'The narrative as a root metaphor for psychology' In Sarbin, T. R. (ed.) *Narrative Psychology* Westport, CT: Praeger

Saunders, P. and Skar, P. (2001) 'Archetypes, complexes and self-organization' *Journal of Analytical Psychology* 46, 3–20

Schopenhauer, A. (1909) *The World as Will and Idea* (vol. III) London: Kegan Paul (Original work published 1844)

—— (1922) *The World as Will and Idea* (vol. I) London: Kegan Paul (Original work published 1844)

Schrag, C. O. (1997) *The Self after Postmodernity* New Haven, CT: Yale University Press

Segal, R. A. (1999) *Theorizing about Myth* Massachusetts, MA: University of Massachusetts Press

Shamdasani, S. (1998) *Cult Fictions* London: Routledge

—— (2003) *Jung and the Making of Modern Psychology* Cambridge: Cambridge University Press

Shope, R. K. (1971) 'Physical and psychic energy' *Philosophy of Science* 38, 1–12

Shotter J (1996) 'Living in a Wittgensteinian world: beyond theory to a poetics of practices' *Journal for the Theory of Social Behaviour* 26, 293–312

—— (1998) 'Social construction and social poetics: Oliver Sacks and the case of Dr P' In Bayer, B. M. and Shotter, J. (eds) *Reconstructing the Psychological Subject* London: Sage

Silberer, H. (1951) 'On symbol-formation' In Rapaport, D. (ed.) *Organization and Pathology of Thought* New York: Columbia University Press (Original work published in 1912)

Sprinker, M. (1980) 'Fictions of the self: the end of autobiography' In Olney, J. (ed.) *Autobiography Essays* Princeton, NJ: Princeton University Press

Stein, M. (1998) *Jung's Map of the Soul* Chicago, IL: Open Court

Sweet, D. (1995) *Heraclitus* Lanham, MD: University Press of America

Tan, S.-L. and Moghaddam, F. M. (1995) 'Reflexive positioning and culture' *Journal for the Theory of Social Behaviour* 25, 387–400

Taylor, C. (1989) *Sources of the Self* Cambridge: Cambridge University Press

Teloh, H. (1976) 'Human nature, psychic energy, and self-actualization in Plato's Republic' *The Southern Journal of Philosophy* XIV (3), 345–58

Thompson, S. (1955) 'Myth and folktales' In Sebeok, T. A. (ed.) *Myth: A Symposium* Bloomington, IN: Indiana University Press

Thouless, R. H. (1951). *General and Social Psychology* (3rd edn) London: University Tutorial Press

Tresan, D. I. (2004) 'This new science of ours: a more or less systematic history of consciousness. Part I' *Journal of Analytical Psychology* 49, 193–216

Trueman, L. (2005) 'The limits of empathy in Jung' *Harvest* 51, 61–72

Tuffin, K. (2005) *Understanding Critical Social Psychology* London: Sage

Turner, V. W. (1967) *The Forest of Symbols* New York: Cornell University Press

Urban, E. (2003) 'Developmental aspects of trauma and traumatic aspects of development' *Journal for Analytical Psychology* 48, 171–90

Valsiner, J. and van der Veer, R. (2000) *The Social Mind* Cambridge: Cambridge University Press

van Fraassen, B. C. (1980) *The Scientific Image* Oxford: Clarendon

van Langenhove, L. and Harré, R. (1993) 'Positioning and autobiography: telling your life' In Coupland, N. and Nussbaum, J. F. (eds) *Discourse and Lifespan Identity* Newbury Park, CA: Sage

Varela, C. R. (1995) 'Ethogenic theory and psychoanalysis: the unconscious as a social construction and a failed explanatory concept' *Journal for the Theory of Social Behaviour* 25, 363–386

Varela, C. R. and Harré, R. (1996) 'Conflicting varieties of realism: causal powers and the problem of social structure' *Journal for the Theory of Social Behaviour* 26, 313–25

Vernon, M. D. (1969) *Human Motivation* Cambridge: Cambridge University Press

Vygotsky, L. (1986) *Thought and Language* Cambridge, MA: The MIT Press (Originally published in 1934)

Wheelwright, P. (1955) 'The semantic approach to myth' In Sebeok, T. A. (ed.) *Myth: A Symposium* Bloomington, IN: Indiana University Press

Wilhelm, R (1950) *I Ching* London: Routledge & Kegan Paul

Wittgenstein, L. (1953) *Philosophical Investigations* Oxford: Blackwell

Worthington, K. L. (1996) *Self as Narrative* Oxford: Clarendon Press

Wundt, W. (1916) *Elements of Folk Psychology* London: George Allen & Unwin

Young, C. and Brook, A. (1994) 'Schopenhauer and Freud' *International Journal of Psychoanalysis* 75, 101–18

Index